Say That We Saw Spain Die

JOHN M. MUSTE

Say That We Saw Spain Die

Literary Consequences
of the Spanish Civil War

Seattle and London

UNIVERSITY OF WASHINGTON PRESS

For Jean

Prefatory Note

A NUMBER of individuals and institutions have assisted me in the writing of this book, and I am indebted to them for whatever virtues it may possess. Frederick J. Hoffman has given me encouragement and advice over a period of years, and this project would never have been completed without his urging. Robert M. Estrich, Roy Harvey Pearce, Robert C. Elliott, Eric Solomon, John Gates, and Moe Fishman have all been helpful in a variety of ways, and they all have my gratitude. The librarians of the University of Wisconsin, the Ohio State University, the Henry E. Huntington Foundation, the University of Colorado, and the New York Public Library were most cooperative. I am also indebted for a grant-in-aid-of-research to the American Council of Learned Societies. Most of all, for her help, her understanding and her patience, I am indebted to my wife, Jean, to whom this book is dedicated.

JOHN M. MUSTE

Acknowledgments

The author would like to express his appreciation to the following:

W. H. Auden, for excerpts from "Spain," by W. H. Auden. Copyright 1937 by W. H. Auden.

Alvah Bessie, for excerpts from *Men in Battle* by Alvah Bessie. Copyright 1939 by Alvah Bessie.

Christopher Cornford, for excerpts from "Full Moon at Tierz: Before the Storming of Huesca," and "Heart of the Heartless World," by John Cornford.

Margot Heinemann, for excerpts from "For R.J.C." and "Grieve in a New Way for New Losses," by Margot Heinemann.

Jack Lindsay, for excerpts from "On Guard for Spain," and "Looking at a Map of Spain on the Devon Coast," by Jack Lindsay.

October House, Inc., for excerpts from "Elegy for Spain" and "Calamiterror," by George Barker.

Harcourt, Brace & World, Inc., for excerpts from *Homage*

Contents

Say That We Saw Spain Die

1. Introduction

I

IN CERTAIN fundamental ways, all war literature recapitulates what has already been said about earlier wars. Sophocles and Thucydides knew that war is destructive and disillusioning, Aristophanes knew that there may be a comic side even to the most tragic events, and Homer knew a great deal about the nature of heroism. In another, equally elementary, sense, every war is unique; and so is its literature. We could not know as much as we do about what makes war fought in the nineteen forties different from all other wars wthout the literary testimony of Norman Mailer, Joseph Heller, and even, save the mark, Leon Uris. We learn from each war's writers the circumstances which make a particular conflict distinctive, and we also learn from them what kind of consciousness and what kind of attitudes were produced by the war and in turn helped to produce its distinctive literature.

The twentieth century has seen two major wars and many minor wars — civil wars, rebellions, coups d'état, police actions, conflicts which are called minor because they killed too few people, not because those who fought in them were immune to misery, shock, pain, or death. Like wars throughout the modern era, most of the conflagrations of our time, major or minor, have been fought on the traditional grounds of national interest, geographical and economic. The extent to which this is true is surprising in view of the importance of politics and political ideas in the modern world. It is no longer possible to argue convincingly that political idealism played any considerable role in the two major struggles of the last fifty years; the bloodletting which began in 1914 and which claimed an entire generation of European manhood has for a long time been recognized by historians as no more than a power struggle between rivals nearly equal in strength and not much different in motivation. What we have chosen to call, with frightening implications, World War II, increasingly takes on much the same lineaments, as the "revisionist" historians do their work and as Josef Stalin becomes a bogeyman even more sinister than Hitler in popular mythology, especially in the United States. We may be unwilling to admit during the Cold War that some of our own present allies in Latin America, Europe, and the Far East may be no more appetizing and no more democratic than the nations behind the Iron Curtain, any more than we were willing to admit during World War II that the Soviet Union was no less oppressive a state than Hitler's Germany, but distance in time has often allowed the people of any nation to judge its erstwhile allies more skeptically. In any case, whatever humanitarian ideas may have been offered at the time, cynically or sincerely, both of our world wars were basically struggles for political power rather than for political ideals.

A genuine political conflict involves the clash of opposing political beliefs, not merely differences of national interests. In this sense, the American Revolution, although obviously economic and national interests played a role (as they always do), was in many ways a political war, and so was the American Civil War, with the same limitations. Clearly enough, a civil war is far more likely to be political in nature than an international conflict, at least in its inception, because those holding political beliefs may decide that only the force of arms will permit them to establish their system within their own countries, and they may therefore have recourse to violence to dispose of political enemies who have held power. But wars between nations are fought by those who already have power in their own nations, almost never to impose a system of political belief upon an alien people. The behavior of the Soviet Union in the years since 1945 is instructive on this point, for the USSR, which, according to its own ideology, should be fighting a revolutionary war all over the globe, in practice has never in this unsettled period seen fit to use its own military establishment to bring its gospel to a new land. It has, of course, used a plethora of other methods in countries outside its immediate orbit, but it has taken direct military action only when its own empire has been threatened from within, as in the Eastern European uprising of 1956.

There was a time when the possibility existed that national wars might go the way of religious crusades and racial incursions in Western society. This was immediately before the first world war, when almost forty years of peace on the European continent and the contemporaneous development of an internationally oriented Socialist movement opened the parallel possibilities that civilized nations might have abandoned war as an instrument of policy and that even if they chose to use force they would have to abandon their choice because working men refused to fight, recognizing that the exploiters (which is to say the rulers) of their own countries were more their enemies than were the common soldiers conscripted by the governments of other nations. The only real possibility of this evaporated when the French and German workers failed to lay down their weapons in 1914.

The rejection of the idea that class lines cut across national boundaries in any decisive way has meant, again, that the political wars of this century have been civil wars. Among these, the Russian Revolution of 1917 with the subsequent conflict between Bolshevik and Tsarist, and the Chinese wars of 1947–49 seem at present to have been the most important, in the sense that they most decisively altered the power structure of the world and the relationships between nations. In both these upheavals, political considerations played a major role, although by no means so exclusive a role as the propagandists of the time and the later official historians would have us believe. But for what we think of as the Western world, and more especially for Great Britain and the United States, it is doubtful whether any other internal conflict has had the intellectual and cultural impact of the Spanish Civil War of 1936–39. This war, in which military action was confined by the borders of Spain, has paradoxically had very little direct influence on the course of modern history, if we conceive of history as the actions and relationships of powerful nations. Six months after the war in Spain ended, the major powers which had tried to influence its outcome were directly involved in a far more widespread and destructive war of their own. Spain itself was left depleted and weak, unable to participate meaningfully in the wider conflict because her resources of men, of industry, of the will to violence had been exhausted.

To understand the effects of the Spanish Civil War and its implications for the attitudes and beliefs of Anglo-American intellectuals, it is necessary to see that war in its context, and to try to recapture, in imagination, the points of view from which contemporaries viewed it. This requires a considerable effort, for if time helps us to see more clearly some aspects of the past, it may also make it more difficult for us to understand others. The essential fact in this case, of course, is the metamorphosis which Anglo-American attitudes toward Marxism and the Soviet Union have undergone in the last two decades. We cannot understand the thirties, nor can we deal sympathetically with its literature and its intellectual attitudes, unless we can put aside, at least temporarily, the psychological attitudes created by the history of the Cold War. We have become so accustomed to regarding Marxism/Leninism and all its works as total evil that most Americans (the British are somewhat less affected by this) find the thirties an almost unbelievable time. Partly this is because during the thirties the "American way of life" our publicists talk about so incessantly came uncomfortably close to disintegrating under economic pressures; partly it is because the thirties were a grim time for most people and they dislike being reminded of grim times; and partly it is because the political agitation and concern which marked our intellectual life in the thirties seem so improbable today.

Marxism was the spark of that agitation and concern, as it was the most powerful political ideology of the first fifty years of this century, until anticolonialism proved a more relevant (if not finally more satisfactory) political idea for peoples whose economic status made Marxism a meaningless abstraction. However repellent the works of Marxism may be to us, it would be pointless to deny its power as the most influential political ideology of the past century. Marxism and Socialism during the thirties seemed to offer a viable solution, in the minds of many intellectuals, to economic and political problems which the older systems seemed entirely unable to cope with. Socialism, so the argument ran, had never had a fair trial in any industrial nation. At worst, it could hardly produce any more disastrous economic situation than the world-wide depression of the thirties, or any worse political conditions than the feeble remonstrances of the "conservative" or "liberal" or "national" governments of the Western powers — Great Britain, France, and the United States — when confronted by the harsh realities of Fascism and Naziism.

Some, of course, were fascinated by what they thought they saw in the Soviet Union: "I have seen the future, and it works." The New Economic Policy and the Five-Year Plans seemed for a while to offer inspiration not only to Keynesian economists and labor leaders but to some of the captains of American industry as well. Others might be disenchanted with the Soviet experiment or with the activities in their own countries of the resident Communist parties, but it was always possible to blame the individuals who made the revolution, rather than the revolution itself. Six years after his brief flirtation with the Party ended, John Dos Passos could still dream that a United Front of Communists, Socialists, Republicans, and Anarchists could sweep aside the forces of reaction and establish a truly democratic socialist society in Spain.

With the economic system running on a single cylinder and apparently ready to break down completely at any time, with the totalitarian governments of Germany and Italy marching unchecked into the Ruhr, and later into Abyssinia, Austria, and Czechoslovakia, the thirties seemed scarcely a time for timidity and restraint. Bright as its promise might have seemed, it was not long before the New Deal seemed too tame to a large part of the intellectual community. Americans who were waiting for the fruits of earth to be distributed equally among all her sons and daughters found Franklin Delano Roosevelt's measures half-hearted and inept. By 1936 the left had all but abandoned hope for the New Deal; radicals could (and did) vote for Roosevelt as a lesser evil than Alf Landon, but they no longer looked to the squire of Hyde Park as the prophet of a new era. He had made it clear enough that his aim was to refurbish the old economic and political system, not to destroy it to make way for a new one. In Great Britain the situation was even more discouraging. A succession of National governments passed in and out of office, Laborite and Tory alike unable to do anything but wring their hands over the problems of unemployment, a restive empire, and a resurgent Germany. No more edifying was the spectacle of France, where Socialist and Nationalist governments took turns at hamstringing each other.

Under such conditions, it is hardly remarkable that a good many intellectuals in both Great Britain and the United States felt compelled to look for drastic solutions. Given the apparent contrast between economic conditions in the United States and western Europe on the one hand, and those in the Soviet Union on the other, it is no more remarkable that many were strongly attracted to communism or to other milder collectivisms. Writers who during the twenties had depicted a decaying society now felt themselves challenged to assist somehow at the birth of a new and better order. Since most of them had no real conception of what that order would be like, they frequently settled, in their books and articles and poems, for literary postmortems on the carcass of the old order. They found new villains in the naïve and selfish middle class who had turned out to be no better than those long-time villains, the malefactors of great wealth; they found new heroes in migrant workers, mill hands, and oppressed Negroes (the union leader as hero was carried over from earlier literature, along with the villainous tycoon). The instruments for their operations were ready to hand in the popular Marxist interpretations of history and society. When it came to dealing with a conflict like the Spanish Civil War, Marx was even more helpful, for

if war inevitably meant violence and bloodshed, Marx had
said that the dictatorship of the proletariat could come only
through violent upheavals. Violence in a good cause could not
be as objectionable as the butchery of World War I, especially
to men who, like many of these writers, had seen violence
and misery on the picket lines in the mill towns and mining
camps.

What they had not seen, however, was modern war in its
later manifestations; what they had not understood was that
politics (whatever ideals are being served) is an activity that
involves intrigue, betrayal, and the multitude of confusions
and compromises which are involved in making it the "art of
the possible." When civilian populations were bombed indis-
criminately, when mass executions wiped out the uninvolved
as well as the guilty, when friends were executed for doctrinal
deviations, when men who had never shot at Franco's Moors
or Foreign Legionaries were given license to shoot soldiers
whose wounds or sickness or disgust had caused them to leave
the trenches, the Spanish Civil War ceased to be the simple
climactic struggle between right and wrong that it had once
seemed to be.

The literature of the Spanish War is important because it
reflects both the idealism and the disillusion of the writers
who had seen it as a holy war. The encounter with violence,
whether at first or second hand, was to change drastically
not only the attitude of British and American writers toward
ideology but their understanding of the nature of violence in
the modern world. The results of this encounter are blindingly
clear in the literature of the second world war and the Korean
conflict, which is so obviously apolitical and whose writers
seem to have gone beyond disillusion to a desperate and consuming nihilism. If the writers of World War II cannot in
any exact sense be called disillusioned, it is because they had

been divested of their illusions before the great war had even begun. And the Spanish Civil War had a great deal to do with the destruction of the political dreams of the thirties, a destruction which left many writers without the props of dogma or ideology when they were almost immediately confronted by a far more widespread and devastating war.

II

The revolt which led to the long and bloody Civil War in Spain broke out on July 16, 1936. The character of the war was determined by a complex of circumstances, some of them peculiar to Spanish history and politics, some of them reflections of the international political situation in the mid-thirties. The kind of ideological war that was waged in Spain, attracting the interest and participation of so many intellectuals of other nations, was possible only in the thirties, since it evoked a special kind of enthusiasm, based on such ideals as the rights of oppressed peoples, the injustice of armed foreign intervention on the side of oppression, and the right of a people to determine their own destiny. The tepid reaction in the "free world" nations to the Hungarian uprising in 1956 or to any of a dozen other disturbances on both sides of the Iron Curtain is evidence enough that we live in a different age. The phrases used to label the issues in the Spanish Civil War are now mostly archaic: fascism versus democracy, fascism versus communism, nationalism versus the Red Peril, Christianity versus communism. Only the last is heard today. But it is also clear that the particular circumstances of the war were possible in Spain alone, with its almost feudal system of land ownership, its powerful Church, its unique susceptibility to anarchism, and its angrily irreconcilable political parties. While Germany in the last years of the Weimar Republic represented one other European nation in which extremist parties on both left and right decisively outweighed the centrist parties, one of these parties was able to seize power and end the republic with little bloodshed. In Spain, the two sides were too evenly matched.

The war broke out in 1936, but its causes lay in the long history of Spanish politics, too long to be gone into here. The more immediate causes lay in the political strife which had begun with the formation of the Spanish Republic in 1932. Since that time, the right- and left-wing parties had alternated at winning elections. The Republicans and their Socialist allies ruled from 1931 until 1933. In 1933 the parties of the right won a parliamentary election and remained in power in a rapidly deteriorating situation through what was called the *"Bienio Negro"* — the black biennium — climaxed by the the revolt of the Asturian miners in 1934 and ending in the resignation of the government in December, 1935. In the elections of February, 1936, the Popular Front coalition (Socialists, Republican Left, Republican Union, and Communists, with the help of Anarchist votes) won a clear majority in the *Cortes*, although it had only a bare majority of the popular vote. The situation was impossible. Those who supported the majority demanded immediate action on its program — reduction of the influence of the Church by withdrawing government subsidies and by taking education out of the hands of the Church, expropriation and distribution among the peasants of the large agricultural holdings of the Church and of the aristocracy, regional autonomy for Catalonia and the Basque provinces, collectivization of industry. But almost half the country had voted for candidates or parties which were unalterably opposed to any of these moves. As a result, the spring of 1936 was chaotic, marked by assassinations and reprisals, strikes, street fights, and increasing hostility on both sides. Attempts at moderation dissatisfied both right and left.

The actual fighting began with a rebellion of regular army officers of a type all too common in Hispanic countries. Careful preparations had been made for a rising against the Popular Front government ever since the 1936 election, and the officers of the army and of the *Guardia Civil*, the national police force, were able to lead a large part of Spain's armed forces in revolt. At first there seemed to be little doubt that the revolution would end quickly in a coup d'état. The government was almost paralyzed; it had been shaky from its inception, helpless to control the violence of extremists on both left and right, and it had no apparent way to combat the uprising. In a number of cities, however, the trade unions and the left-wing parties took the initiative, demanding that the government open the armories and arsenals and supply them with weapons. After some hesitation (in one day three premiers held office briefly: the first two were dismissed when they failed to act quickly to arm the popular militias)[1] the arms were distributed. In Madrid and Barcelona these makeshift armies defeated insurgent units of the Army and the Civil Guard, and large areas of Spain remained under the nominal control of the Republican government.

In fact, however, the government in Madrid had less control over most of its territory than did Workers' Committees, made up largely of members of the left-wing parties and the trade unions, chiefly the Anarchist CNT (*Confederación Nacional de Trabajo*) and the Socialist UGT (*Union General de Trabajadores*). This development had its ironical side. The avowed purpose of the Insurgent uprising was to prevent a revolution from the left, but in the chaotic aftermath of the July uprising a real revolution took place in many parts of Loyalist Spain. In the Anarchist stronghold of Barcelona, fac-

[1] Hugh Thomas, *The Spanish Civil War* (London: Eyre & Spottiswoode, 1961), pp. 142–44.

tories were taken over and run by the workers; in Catalonia and other rural areas, large estates were expropriated and divided up among the peasantry. This revolution was accompanied by considerable bloodshed, much of it directed against the Church. None of this violence had government approval, but the Loyalist regime did not truly govern until October. With all the violence, the period from July until October was one of considerable freedom and happiness for people unused to either, one of the few periods in any country's history when "the workers . . . became the real rulers of the country."[2] If the government was to last, however, such an anarchic situation could not be tolerated for long, and after October, 1936, Madrid had an increasingly strong hold over the part of Spain held by the Loyalists.

While the revolution of the workers was going on inside Loyalist territory, the Insurgents had been steadily reducing the size of that territory. The revolt had originated in Morocco, and its early strongholds on the mainland were in the South and in the region of Aragon in the North. During the summer and early fall of 1936, the Insurgent armies consolidated their position in the South by capturing Malaga, an important seaport on the Mediterranean, and Badajoz on the Portuguese frontier, where one of the most notorious mass executions of the war was carried out in the bull ring. Toledo, in the central highlands, was captured by the Insurgents, ending the famous siege of the Alcazar. By October the offensive had reached the outskirts of Madrid, and it once again seemed inevitable that the war would soon end with an Insurgent triumph.

At Madrid the offensive stalled. Aided by inept Insurgent tactics and by important numbers of foreign volunteers and armaments, the Loyalist army succeeded in turning back the

[2] Gerald Brenan, *The Spanish Labyrinth* (New York: Macmillan Co., 1943), p. 317.

Moors and Foreign Legionaries. At this point the battle lines became relatively stable and definite for the first time, and both sides settled down for a long war. On some fronts there was little action for months at a time; George Orwell has written about such an area in *Homage to Catalonia*. Both sides were able to develop their defenses, by installing trenches, command posts and artillery emplacements, and they proceeded to mount the offensives and counteroffensives that provided so much information for the strategists and tacticians of World War II.

By the end of 1936, the opponents had staked out their respective territories, and the war maps had taken on the outlines they were to retain through most of the war. The Loyalists retained control of the Mediterranean coast from the French border to a point south of Almería. In the North, around Teruel, the Insurgents had advanced to within about seventy miles of the sea in a salient which would eventually divide the Loyalist territory; south of Madrid a Loyalist salient reached to within sixty miles of the Portuguese border. Most of the southern, western, and northern regions were in the hands of the Insurgents, who had established their capital at Burgos. Only a pocket in the North along the Bay of Biscay, containing the cities of Oviedo, Gijon, Santander, and Bilbao, remained in Loyalist hands. Some of the fiercest fighting of the war resulted from Insurgent attempts to reduce this pocket, but because few foreigners fought in the area it is mentioned only infrequently in the literature of the war. C. Day Lewis' *The Nabarra* and various commentaries on the famous bombing of Guernica are the only noteworthy discussions of this isolated segment of the war.

The fighting around Madrid was the focus of military action. By the time the Insurgents were able to mount a full-scale attack on the city in November, 1936, the opportunity for a quick and easy victory had passed. The Loyalists had begun to organize their forces, munitions were arriving from Russia, and the foreign volunteers were providing reinforcements for the army. The ability of the Loyalists to hold Madrid (in the end, it was the last important city to surrender) provided a rallying cry and an important psychological lift. In addition, the city was of great strategic importance. Had Madrid fallen, the Insurgents would have had a clear path east to Valencia and could probably have mopped up the Mediterranean coast at their leisure. But the Loyalists did hold Madrid; they were even able, at Guadalajara, to mount a successful offensive against Italian troops and thus to ensure a long struggle. Even so, the eventual outcome was never really in doubt to those who viewed the war realistically. Russia was too far away and too stingy to provide enough equipment to offset the contributions of men and materiel which the Insurgents received from Germany and Italy. France, Great Britain, and the United States, for various reasons, provided almost no help at all for the Loyalists. Great Britain, at times, seemed more friendly to Franco than to the Loyalists. The fighting continued until March, 1939, but the outcome of the war had been settled long before that, in places remote from the scenes of battle.

The importance of foreign intervention in causing the Spanish Civil War is a matter of permanent dispute. Historians sympathetic to the Franco regime have claimed that the Insurgent uprising was an attempt to forestall a plot to communize all of Spain, under directions from Moscow.[3] Most observers, however, taking into account the very small size of the Communist party in Spain and its tiny representation in the *Cortes*, are inclined to doubt that such a plot, even if it existed, was a real menace to Spain. Historians sympathetic to

[3] For example, Robert Sencourt, *Spain's Ordeal* (London: Longmans, Green & Co., 1939).

the Loyalists, on the other hand, point an accusing finger at the machinations of dissident generals, citing evidence that they had been negotiating with Hitler and Mussolini at least as early as 1934 and that their revolt had received promises of support from these sources. It seems likely, in view of the Spanish political situation discussed earlier, that foreign intrigues were not decisive in starting the war; there was provocation aplenty in Spain itself.[4]

Once the war was well started, foreign intervention played an increasingly important and ultimately decisive role. The Burgos regime received help in the form of armaments from Italy and Germany, and substantial groups of volunteers from the Italian army were shipped to Spain to bolster Insurgent forces.[5] Gerald Brenan, who comes as close to objectivity in reporting the Spanish War as any writer, compared the support received by the two sides, commenting on its significance:

> The decisive factor in the war was . . . the foreign intervention. Germany and Italy supported the rebel generals from the start. Stalin only decided to intervene in September. It should be noted that there was a difference in their method of doing so. The Fascist dictators dealt directly with Franco and his generals and sent their war materials to them. Although they encouraged the Falangists, they never made them their representatives in Spain, but . . . kept them as a lever for putting pressure on the government. Stalin, on the other hand, saw to it that the arms which he supplied and the International Brigades which he organized should secure the predominance of the Communist Party. They alone could be trusted to look after Soviet interests.[6]

Soviet policy was successful in dominating the Loyalist government because that government had no other place to

---

[4] David T. Cattell, *Communism and the Spanish Civil War* (Berkeley: University of California Press, 1955), pp. 35–45.

[5] F. Jay Taylor, *The United States and the Spanish Civil War* (New York: Bookman Associates, 1956), p. 65.

[6] Brenan, *The Spanish Labyrinth*, p. 323.

turn for weapons and supplies. The Congress of the United States, acting under pressure from President Franklin D. Roosevelt and against the urgent advice of Claude Bowers, the ambassador to Spain, had passed the Neutrality Act, which embargoed shipments of arms to either belligerent. Great Britain, led by Neville Chamberlain, was urging on the nations of Europe a Non-Intervention Agreement. When the agreement was arrived at, Great Britain assiduously held to it and forced France to join her. Germany and Italy blandly joined in calling for neutrality while they kept a steady flow of arms and men moving to Franco and lent the support of their naval units whenever it seemed necessary. France, with a Popular Front government led by Leon Blum, was sympathetic to Spain, but under the pressure brought by Great Britain was forced to restrict its aid to the Loyalists to turning a blind eye to the passage of men and materiel across the Pyrenees.

The circumstances provided a golden opportunity for the Soviet Union. The worst motives could be (and were) ascribed to the actions of the United States, Great Britain, and France — an example of this line is the series of dispatches sent by Ernest Hemingway to *Ken*[7] — while the USSR could adopt the pose of the only friend of Spanish democracy. On the world scene, this meant that Stalin could divert attention from the Moscow trials and recoup whatever propaganda losses his regime had suffered through those trials. At the same time, the war in Spain represented an opportunity to test Russian planes, tanks, and guns in action without risking much loss of prestige if those who used the arms should be defeated, and to provide an exercise in tactics and strategy for promising young officers. Once it had become apparent that the Loyalist government was not going to collapse quickly, the Soviet

[7] Ernest Hemingway; dispatches published biweekly in *Ken*, April 7, 1938, through September 22, 1938.

Union saw an opportunity to establish a considerable measure of control over that government, with a chance to dominate Spain when the war ended, in the unlikely event that the Loyalists should win. By insisting that all aid sent should be paid for with gold from the reserves of the Spanish treasury, the Soviet Union could assure itself a financially successful investment.

In the United States and Great Britain, the effect of the Soviet aid and the official policies of the British and American governments was to arouse considerable sympathy for the Loyalist cause. The Communist parties of the two countries, of course, made as much capital as possible out of the situation. A good many people were convinced that official refusal to give any aid whatever to the legal, democratically elected government of Spain (this was always emphasized) constituted a betrayal of democracy. Since "democracy" had been betrayed before during the thirties, in China and in Abyssinia, it seemed even more necessary to draw the line in Spain. Governmental neutrality and public apathy only strengthened the convictions of those who saw the Loyalists as the last best hope of democracy. The intelligentsia once more set out to save the world from itself. Twenty years later Congressmen would call them "excessive premature anti-fascists."

The nature of foreign intervention in Spain and the actual conduct of the war helped to determine the outcome, but there was a third important factor which helped assure the eventual triumph of the Insurgents. This third cause was the debilitating political infighting which went on behind the Loyalist lines, occasionally leading to revolutions within revolutions which clearly did the Loyalist cause no good. The struggle for power within the Loyalist government arose from a complex set of causes: ancient political rivalries, the insistence of the Soviet Union on an important role for its representatives, various regional rivalries, and the exigencies of trying to win the war.

In this contest for power, the greatly strengthened Communist party played a vital part. The Communists controlled the International Brigades, and the activities of the foreign volunteers were exploited by the Party's propaganda apparatus to provide another lever for dominating the Loyalist government. Furthermore, the Communists were able to form an alliance with the strong Socialist party. Francisco Largo Caballero, the leader of the Socialists, was as pleased at the opportunity to ally his party with the viceroys of Stalin as he had been when *Pravda* hailed him as the "Spanish Lenin." [8] Together the Socialists and the Communists were able to control the Loyalist government through most of the war.

Winning the war was, of course, the expressed aim of all the parties in Loyalist Spain, but there was little agreement on how this was to be accomplished. The Communist-Socialist coalition favored a strong central government with full power over all Loyalist armed forces, and when this coalition gained power in the fall of 1936 the government immediately moved to strengthen its position. It called for the dissolution of the union and party militias which had done most of the fighting in the early days of the war. These militias would be incorporated into a national army under a centralized command, in whose operations the unions and the parties would have no voice. The government also called for the return of expropriated private property to its owners.

This action had two important objectives. It would weaken the most important opponents of a strong central government, the Catalonian Anarchists, by withdrawing the measure of autonomy which they had established in their stronghold, and

[8] Brenan, *The Spanish Labyrinth*, pp. 302–05, 319–22; Thomas, *The Spanish Civil War*, pp. 98–99.

would thus end the only real challenge to the domination of the Socialist-Communist coalition. The economic side of the program would enable the government to depict Loyalist Spain as the perfect nonrevolutionary bourgeois democracy, one which took special care to safeguard the rights of private property. At the same time, such a move would gain the support of the large Catalonian bourgeoisie in the struggle to end Anarchist domination of the northeast. A secondary benefit of the two-point program would be the chance to suppress troublesome minority parties which were certain to oppose both the military and the economic proposals.[9]

One of the ways in which the government implemented its military policy was to refuse to send weapons and ammunition to the party militias. Since the Communist party controlled the distribution of Soviet arms, it could make certain that only the units of the Popular Army would be properly equipped. In addition, the government set out to depict those who refused to abandon the militia system as disloyal to the Republic and as allies of the Insurgents. The resentment aroused by this program certainly did not help the Loyalist war effort. In some places, attempts to implement the program led to fighting. The most serious incident took place in Barcelona in May, 1937, when government troops and militiamen of the POUM (*Partido Obrero de Unificación Marxista*), a small dissident party, battled in the streets for three days. The latter part of George Orwell's *Homage to Catalonia* describes this battle. There was also some trouble with militia units at the front whose members objected to being denied arms and ammunition.

The question of political activity on the Loyalist side is too complex to be discussed here in much detail, although it is of great importance in the history of the war. The drive for

[9] Brenan, *The Spanish Labyrinth*, pp. 317–21.

a strong central government was the chief cause of trouble, and it still raises very difficult problems. The attempt to unify the armed forces was certainly not illogical. It is extremely unlikely that modern war can be fought successfully by independent armies whose commanders are responsible to no central authority. Even Orwell, who suffered for his part in opposing the government's program, admitted that central control was necessary. And there is probably a good deal to be said for the government's attempt to return private property to its owners. Only by doing so could it hope to gain the support of the Spanish middle class and to placate the foreign owners of property in Spain, which might increase the government's chances of getting aid from Great Britain and the United States. On the other hand, the harsh treatment of the party militias and the fact that government control had to be asserted, in some instances, by force caused considerable resentment and a consequent loss of enthusiasm. Even worse, for many, was the increasing influence of the Communist party, far out of proportion to its prewar strength. It may well be that the Loyalists' political problems were insoluble. It is certain that the attempts to solve these problems helped the Insurgents more than the Loyalists.

The Insurgents also had political problems, but they were not so serious. The important right-wing parties — the Falangists, the Monarchists, and the Carlists — had different aims, but the army was firmly in control. In the spring of 1937 there was a move among the Falangists to institute immediate social reforms in Insurgent territory, along the lines of a program originally proposed by the group's founder, José Antonio Primo de Rivera, son of the late dictator. The program was considerably more radical than that of the Communist party. The Army easily quashed this move, however, and Franco was able to tighten his grip by decreeing a merger of the three major parties in a new Falange, with himself as its leader.

Not until the summer of 1938 was there any further trouble on the Insurgent side. Then, late in the war, some resentment developed against the influence of Italy and Germany. A few officers suggested that it would be better to negotiate with the Loyalists than to continue to accept aid from allies who would certainly extract a high price for their support. Brenan believes that an armistice might have been possible if the British had put pressure on Hitler at this point. This is pure speculation, but there is little question that both sides were by this time thoroughly sick of war. In any case, the moment passed, and when Russia withdrew her support of the Loyalists in September, 1938, there was no more agitation for a truce on the Insurgent side. Complete victory was too close at hand.[10]

The international ramifications of the conflict were of surpassing importance in determining its course, and there was little doubt, from the very early days of the war, about which side was receiving the more effective aid. The fact that the war continued as long as it did can be attributed to the aid that reached Loyalist Spain, from Russia and in lesser amounts from France and Mexico, the popular support which the government could rely upon, at least in the early part of the war, and the blundering of the Insurgents. There is good reason to believe that if the generals had earlier established a unified command (Franco did not achieve undisputed mastery until the summer of 1937) and had integrated their strategy with more effectiveness they might have won the war much more quickly. But in the end only the most incredible stupidity could have frittered away the tremendous advantages the Insurgents possessed.

Even a brief review of the history of the war and some of the determinants of that history help explain the particular

10 Brenan, *The Spanish Labyrinth*, pp. 330–31.

character of the literature of the Spanish Civil War, especially of that written by Loyalist sympathizers. The heavy military superiority of the Insurgents and the fact that they were supported by Mussolini's Italy and Hitler's Germany account both for the apocalyptic view of the war adopted by many writers and for the note of desperation so common in their work. If this was to be the final battle for righteousness against the forces of evil, Loyalist sympathizers saw the victory of what they regarded as evil as being very nearly inevitable. This attitude helps make the literature of the Spanish Civil War both hortatory and tragic.[11]

III

There can be little doubt about the strength of Marxist influence during the thirties. The statistics reflecting the reawakened interest in Communism are impressive,[12] but they give no hint of the excitement of the times, the parades and the mass meetings and committees and projects and congresses which engaged the attention of writers and other intellectuals. When the Spanish Civil War erupted, American writers were virtually unanimous in sympathizing with the Loyalists.[13] It is im-

[11] By far the best history of the conflict is Hugh Thomas's *The Spanish Civil War*. Despite occasional errors in detail, Thomas presents a thoroughly documented and remarkably objective history of the entire war. Other helpful books on the subject, in addition to the works already cited, include the following: David T. Cattell, *Soviet Diplomacy and the Spanish Civil War* (Berkeley: University of California Press, 1957); James Cleugh, *Spain in the Modern World* (London: Eyre & Spottiswoode, 1952); Robert G. Colodny, *The Struggle for Madrid* (New York: Paine-Whitman, 1958); Salvador de Madariaga, *Spain: A Modern History* (New York: Frederick Praeger, 1958); Allen Guttmann, *The Wound in the Heart: America and the Spanish Civil War* (Glencoe, Ill.: The Free Press of Glencoe, 1962); and Robert Payne, ed., *The Civil War in Spain* (New York: G. P. Putnam's Sons, 1962).

[12] Walter B. Rideout, *The Radical Novel in the United States, 1900–1954* (Cambridge: Harvard University Press, 1956), pp. 139–49.

[13] *Writers Take Sides* (New York: League of American Writers, 1938). Of 413 responses listed, 406 express sympathy for the Loyalists, though

portant to note, however, that they differed in the reasons for their response and in the depth and strength of their commitments to the various ideologies of the time.

The motives that drew men to Spain were for the most part the same motives that had drawn them to radical politics in the first place: an altruistic desire for a world in which poverty, injustice, and misery might be eliminated, combined in varying degrees with a desire for power, an urge to lose oneself in an historical movement that would provide an identity the individual felt unable to establish, and anger and bitterness at the dominant social and political system and one's own place in it. When Alvah Bessie wrote that "the historical event of Spain had coincided with a long-felt compulsion to complete the destruction of the training I had received all through my youth" and went on to give the desire to "achieve self-integration" as the first of his two major reasons for going to Spain,[14] he was being unusually honest, but the motives he describes were not unusual. Spain was in some ways a special event. It provided a focus for the revolutionary drives of many men, but did not change their motivations. Many writers had joined the Writers' Congress or had helped out in strikes for the same reasons.

This is not to say that the men who went to Spain were dilettantes. Getting to Spain between July, 1936, and the autumn of 1938 required perseverance, courage, and (usually) the friendship of an official in the Communist party, which had the most efficient apparatus for getting people into Spain.[15]

---

in some cases with definite reservations about Stalinist influence on the Republican government; six were termed neutral; only one expressed sympathy with Franco. A similar poll taken in England showed similar results.

[14] Alvah Bessie, *Men in Battle* (New York: Veterans of the Abraham Lincoln Brigade, 1954), p. 182.

[15] Murray Kempton, *Part of Our Time: Some Monuments and Ruins of the Thirties* (New York: Simon & Schuster, 1955), p. 313.

The journey has been described by several writers. It required the guile to convince the State Department that one had no intention of going to Spain, the money to get to Paris, and some kind of entrée to the recruiting offices there. From Paris in the early days of the war, the next step was transportation to Marseilles and an ocean trip to Alicante or Valencia;[16] the presence in the Mediterranean of German submarines and warships made such a journey hazardous. In the later days the journey from Paris meant a trip on foot across the Andorras, an exhausting and dangerous passage,[17] for by 1938 it was too dangerous to use the sea routes. Once in Spain, volunteers in the Republican Army made themselves automatically liable to loss of British or American citizenship; they received the sketchiest training and then went into battle poorly equipped.[18] Of the three thousand Americans who joined Loyalist forces, only twelve hundred left Spain alive, and most of those had been wounded at least once. The British volunteers had no better luck. This was hardly a war for dilettantes.

The hazards of getting to Spain were somewhat less for those who went first as accredited correspondents and then decided to volunteer, but there were not a great many who did this. There were not even a very great many correspondents in Spain, despite occasional books and articles which seem to indicate that they outnumbered the entire population of Spain. The hazards were great enough even for the correspondents;

16 John Sommerfield, *Volunteer in Spain* (New York: Alfred A. Knopf, 1937), pp. 13–14.

17 Bessie, *Men in Battle*, pp. 7–24.

18 Despite Russian aid, the Loyalists never had enough arms or ammunition, and what they had was usually next to useless. Late in the war, the International Brigade Bulletins were discussing the use of antitank rifle bullets and the use of rifle fire as a defense against aircraft. (Kempton, *Part of Our Time*, p. 311). See references to this situation also in Sommerfield, Bessie, Orwell's *Homage to Catalonia* (Boston: Beacon Press, 1952), and Hemingway's *For Whom the Bell Tolls*.

they had to contend with bombing raids and with the secret police, both of which tended to be capricious and often fatal. Few correspondents chose to increase the hazards by following the examples of George Orwell and Jim Lardner.

All of this indicates that the men who went to Spain to fight were strongly committed to some ideology. But such a statement requires qualification; they were not all committed to the same set of ideals, nor were their commitments equally firm. One of the reasons for the widespread disillusion brought about by experience in the Spanish Civil War was the fact that many of the volunteers in Spain experienced their first encounter with real military and political discipline and with bureaucratic stupidity. If most of the Britons and Americans who got to Spain were members of or sympathizers with the Communist party, others were Socialists, Trotskyists, Anarchists, or simply republicans. Non-Communist volunteers could hardly help but be dismayed by the increasing control which the Communists exercised over the Republican government and the methods with which that control was enforced.[19] And even Communists themselves could be disturbed by the harsh discipline of the battlefield police and the political conformity enforced as part of the military order.

The violence of the war proved a shock to almost all of the volunteers. Few were old enough to have seen the first world war, and whatever education they had had at home in the horrors of war could hardly have prepared them for a struggle in which tanks, bombing planes, and other "improved" weapons to be used in World War II made their appearance. No war

[19] John Gates has told me that Socialist volunteers simply left the Brigades when Communist control became too onerous, and that the activities of the battlefield police may have been greatly exaggerated (Conversation, February 22, 1958). He maintained that only two Americans, both three-time deserters, were executed in Spain during the entire Civil War. If Gates is correct, the stories of such activities form the most persistent myth of the Spanish War.

pictures or plays or novels could have prepared them for the destruction they saw. Finally these men were fighting in a lost cause. All the killing, the destruction, the intrigue, the executions, might be stomached if they brought improved conditions to Spain and the satisfaction of triumph to the volunteers. But as the war progressed and it became increasingly clear that for a variety of reasons the Insurgents were bound to triumph, the bitterness of defeat infected not only the soldiers but a great many others who had never seen Spain but had committed themselves to the Loyalist cause.

The commitment to the Loyalists took many different forms among literary men. A good many went to fight, and a number of them died: Ralph Fox, Christopher St. John Sprigg, Jim Lardner, Charles Donnelly, and John Cornford among them. Others like Ernest Hemingway and Stephen Spender, and such journalists as Herbert Matthews and Vincent Sheean, went to Spain and gave encouragement to the Loyalists and also helped through writing and speaking to raise money for the cause in their own countries. Such other writers as Day Lewis, W. H. Auden (his single visit to Spain was very brief), Jack Lindsay, Norman Rosten, and Edna St. Vincent Millay generated considerable enthusiasm for the Loyalist cause without real firsthand knowledge of the war. Still others, including Kenneth Rexroth, John Malcolm Brinnin, and George Barker, expressed interest in the struggle and sympathy for the Loyalists without seeming to feel a violent partisanship. In the face of all this variety, it is difficult to make generalizations about commitment. At the same time it is perfectly clear, from the fact that all of the writers named above and a great many others besides wrote about the Spanish War out of sympathy for the cause, that political belief had an important role in the literature of the thirties, and that it is an important aspect of the literature of the Spanish Civil War.

There were other variations in the nature of commitment. Such writers as Granville Hicks, V. F. Calverton, and Mike Gold felt that a commitment to Marxism involved also the acceptance of a Marxist view of literature. In effect, this meant that literature became a weapon in the class war, and that the value of any piece of literature depended upon its usefulness to the cause. In practice those who accepted this interpretation tended to use their writings to reflect the Party line, and to heap scorn on writers whose work showed defeatist or Trotskyist or diversionist tendencies. Such writers as Jack Lindsay, Tom Wintringham, John Cornford, Edwin Rolfe, Upton Sinclair, and John Howard Lawson viewed the Spanish Civil War from such a position; even a confirmed Communist like Alvah Bessie was sternly taken to task for the "defeatism" of his book *Men in Battle*.[20]

Other writers felt less committed to a specifically Communist position, and could therefore write from a more general concern for the human problems created by the Spanish War, as they had written from less doctrinaire viewpoints about other dilemmas of the thirties. Kenneth Rexroth, Stephen Spender, John Dos Passos, and George Barker are all clearly on the side of the Loyalists, but in various ways they all subject the war to private interpretations.

The causes for the disillusionment which overtook many of these writers as the result of the Spanish Civil War have been mentioned before. The causes seemed to operate equally on men who had actually fought in Spain, on those who had seen the war at first hand without actually fighting in it, and on those whose contact with it was never intimate. The kind of

[20] Conversation with John Gates. Bessie was evidently reprimanded by the Party, but according to Gates other veterans of the war felt that his picture had been honest and accurate. Ironically, in another context Bessie was among the accusers in the Party trial of Albert Maltz for the same crime. (Kempton, *Part of Our Time*, p. 201)

commitment also seems to have had little influence on the
results of a knowledge of violence. Both Kenneth Rexroth,
who never got within three thousand miles of the Spanish War,
and George Orwell, who fought and was wounded in it, had
been independent radicals before 1936, and neither changed
in the years after 1940. Edwin Rolfe, John Sommerfield, and
Tom Wintringham all fought in Spain and all remained as
devoted to communism as did Jack Lindsay, John Howard
Lawson, or Alexander Saxton. George Barker and W. H.
Auden may not have had much direct knowledge of the war,
but they turned away from political themes as sharply as
Stephen Spender and Ernest Hemingway.

The fact of violence, however, was of great importance to
those who wrote about the Spanish Civil War, and it is in the
variety of responses to this fact that the question of commitment assumes importance. In the pages that follow, it should
be clear that for some writers ideology provided a means of
ordering violence, of somehow making it comprehensible and
acceptable. In John Sommerfield's *Volunteer in Spain* and in
the poetry of men like Jack Lindsay, the ideology works pretty
well. The result may not be (in fact, is not) great literature,
but the thought that the killing and the destruction of the war
in Spain would lead to a new society permitted the writer to
believe that the killing was justified. Most of the literature
which reflects this tendency was produced in 1936 or 1937,
when history could still be thought to be headed for a Loyalist
victory.

As the war progressed, as the destruction became worse
and the hope for a Loyalist victory more and more forlorn,
ideology's magic powers began to fade. In the poems of Edwin
Rolfe, in Ernest Hemingway's *For Whom the Bell Tolls*, in
such a play as Maxwell Anderson's *Key Largo*, attempts were
still being made (in the latter two, after the end of the war)

to contain the war in some kind of ideological pattern which would give it meaning. But the statements of ideals in these productions lack conviction; they have become rhetorical and hollow, and the invocations of ideological gods no longer have much effect. Rolfe, in one of his poems, invokes the Loyalist heroine *La Pasionaria* much as does the boy Joaquin in Hemingway's novel, but with no more effect. Joaquin turns his prayers to the Virgin Mary, and Rolfe returns his horrified gaze to a ruined city.

The destruction of the Marxian myth of history in the context of the Spanish Civil War evoked various responses. The poet Charles Donnelly tried to contain his knowledge of death in a hard irony, and had considerable success in the two poems he wrote before he himself was killed; they have some resemblance to Randall Jarrell's poems of the second world war. George Orwell, writing after his own participation in the war had ended, had similar success in describing the Spanish War from a skeptical belief in humanity that had little in common with Marxism. These men, and a very few others, found a means of ordering violence. But there were others, among whom Stephen Spender is the most famous, who simply registered death, and who seem to have become increasingly appalled and disoriented by their increasing knowledge of horror. Some of Spender's poems and those of John Lepper, T. A. R. Hyndman, Sylvia Townsend Warner, and Herbert Read, as well as Robert Payne's novel *The Song of the Peasant* and Alvah Bessie's *Men in Battle*, are simply records of disaster.

The diminishing ability of ideology to provide a useful literary means of ordering violence follows a roughly chronological course. While it is true that a literature of total disillusion was being produced during most of the war, and that after the war had ended some writers were still trying to ex-

plain their experiences in ideological terms, it is also true
that a general progression from innocence to experience can
be traced in this literature. This is a progression which has
profound significance in the history of modern literature. The
literature of innocence is closely related to the proletarian literature of the thirties, to the novels, poems, and plays of
social protest and political agitation. The literature of experience, dealing with the same war and in some cases with identical events, is far more distant from the literature of innocence
than from the literature of the first and second world wars.

The Spanish Civil War provided the first violent test, at
least for most Britons and Americans, of the usefulness of
Marxism as a means of ordering experience. If a good many
writers had accepted Marxism, with more or less enthusiasm,
it was because this ideology offered a means of comprehending
the catastrophes of the modern world, and because it offered
assurances that turmoil could have a purpose. In its twentieth-
century manifestations Marxism seemed to offer intellectuals
in general and writers in particular the opportunity to help
direct the course of events, to be a part of history. But Marxism
is, among other things, a doctrine which exalts violence as a
necessary means of evolution.

The writers who accepted this notion, even reveled in it,
had often witnessed no more bloody incidents than those attendant on Union Square brawls. Some of these were bloody
enough, but they hardly involved mass slaughter or the deaths
of dozens of women and children. Ella Mae Wiggins could
be a martyr only because she didn't die with a hundred other
women. The writers who had seen no more than this were on
the whole unprepared for what they were to learn from the
war in Spain. A strike or a riot can be violent and destructive,
but only very rarely to the same degree as bombings, strafings,
or mass execution. As Frederick J. Hoffman has shown con-

vincingly, the scale of violence directly affects the nature of our response to it.[21] The writers who went to Spain found out that war and revolution are destructive, that even Marxists are often inefficient bureaucrats, and that history does not always move in expected directions. The pressure of the new knowledge was too much for most of these writers to withstand.

The fundamental importance of the Spanish Civil War in the literature of the United States and Great Britain is in the fact that it was a major element in the almost complete destruction of one of the means by which modern writers have attempted to order their knowledge of a violent and chaotic world. Other factors were, of course, important: the Moscow Trials, the Nazi-Soviet Pact of 1939, the infighting within the left-wing movements in both countries.[22] The war in Spain was not an isolated event. But it was the event which buried the idea that a new revolutionary doctrine could provide a way to order chaotic experience as other religious and political doctrines had done in the past. Our literature underwent a decisive change when the Spanish Civil War showed that Marxism would not bear the weight of this task.

[21] *The Mortal No: Death and the Modern Imagination* (Princeton: Princeton University Press, 1964).

[22] Daniel Aaron's *Writers on the Left* (New York: Harcourt, Brace & World, 1961) makes a thorough study of the stormy romance between American intellectuals and the Communist party.

2. The Sky Is Aflame

IN THE first excitement of the Spanish Civil War, the literary mood of the writers who felt themselves involved, whether in physical fact or in spirit, was militant and combative. All through the thirties the "Fascist" nations (Germany, Italy, Japan) had been seizing whatever territory seemed most ripe for the picking, and with no more than token opposition from the "democracies." Now, in Spain, the forces of evil were once again at work, but at last they were being resisted. Clearly the duty of writers was to sound the call to arms, to show the virtues of the good guys and the evil of the bad — in short, to propagandize.

This presented no very difficult task for the numerous writers who had acquired certain skills as experts in "agit-prop," nor for the writers who might have no formal connection with the Communist party but whose interest in and sympathy for the causes of the Left had been developing throughout the thirties. They had written for *The New Masses* or *Left Review* or any of a dozen other magazines in England and the United States and on the continent. After July, 1936, the war in Spain provided a new subject. The most blatantly propagandistic writing was turned out by such writers as Jack Lindsay, an English Communist who never went to Spain during the war, but whose poetry reflects no uncertainty about the merits of the struggle. Lindsay's poems try to make it perfectly clear that the Insurgents were no better than snakes, and that the Spanish Republic was defended by brave and heroic men. Other minor poets could work themselves into transports of poetic wrath merely by reading newspaper reports and attending mass meetings, but few of them could match Lindsay for fervor and poetic blood lust.

Lindsay's technique consists largely of piling up ugly images to describe the heroes and villains of his poems. One opus, "Looking at a Map of Spain on the Devon Coast," provides a sample:

> The brittle mask has broken, the money-mask
> that hid the jackal jaws, the mask of fear
> that twisted the tender face of love; and eyes
> now look on naked eyes. The map of Spain
> seethes with the truth of things, no longer closed
> in greed's geography, an abstract space
> of imports, exports, capitalist statistics,
> the jargon record of a tyrannous bargain.
> The scroll of injustice, the sheet of paper is torn,
> and behind the demolished surface of the lie
> the Spanish people are seen with resolute faces,
> They break the dark grilles
> on custom's stuccoed wall
> and come into the open.[1]

There is much more than this, ending with the poet's self-conscious gesture, "I stand at the atlantic (*sic*) edge and look

[1] Jack Lindsay, "Looking at a Map of Spain on the Devon Coast," in *Poems for Spain*, Stephen Spender and John Lehmann, eds. (London: Hogarth Press, 1939), p. 61.

southwards and raise my hand to Spain. Salute."[2] This poem, like so many other poems, articles, novels, plays, and manifestoes relies on images of violence combined with the jargon of left-wing propaganda to produce its emotional effect. The references to "the truth of things," "the scroll of injustice," and "the Spanish people . . . with resolute faces" are vague, and the images are overwrought. One has difficulty constructing a mental image of a map which is seething with truth.

Another of Lindsay's poems about Spain is one of the longest written about the war. It was called a "mass declamation," intended for performance by a chanting chorus at rallies in support of the Loyalists. Lindsay maintains that it was performed "many hundreds of times in those years all over Britain," but its chief function was at the big London meetings: "The usual thing for the main meetings in support of the Spanish people was a programme with speeches by say Gollancz, Harry Pollitt and the Dean of Canterbury (or Duchess of Atholl) plus On Guard."[3] The popularity of such productions encouraged Lindsay to believe that he had discovered a new genre, which would serve the purpose of establishing a poetry written by intellectuals but comprehensible to the masses.[4] Despite Lindsay's optimistic view of the masses' receptiveness to poetry, the evident apathy of the British working class to the Spanish conflict makes it clear that his mass declamations appealed, if at all, only to the intellectual and artistic left-wingers.

"On Guard for Spain" itself is a bombastic exercise of some three hundred and fifty lines,[5] a riot of exhortation and images

[2] *Ibid.*, p. 64.

[3] Lindsay, undated letter to author, *ca.* June, 1957.

[4] Lindsay, "A Plea for Mass Declamation," *Left Review*, III (October, 1937), 511–17.

[5] Lindsay, "On Guard for Spain," *Left Review*, III (March, 1937), 81–84.

of blood and ravening wolves and evil crawling out of slimy holes. It is a kind of apotheosis of the militant propagandist poem, with its incredibly noble heroes and its absolutely evil villains, and it accepts and passes on myths of the Spanish War which had already gained currency. Two short passages will give the flavor of the poem, but only a reading of the complete work can demonstrate its true quality:

> A mailed fist of thunder struck down that sun of hope,
> and in the deliberate darkness the murderers move.
> Out of the barracks of conspiracy
> were led the hoodwinked soldiers.
> Gold was silently spilt
> to grease the wheels of counter-revolution.
> Those dumps of reaction, the arsenal churches,
> bared their armories of oppression.
> The fascist monster, slimed from the night,
> roared out over Spain.
>
> On guard, Spain, on guard!
>
> * * * * * * * *
>
> I rose from the bed of my wife's young body
> at the call of Liberty.
> O feed with my blood the flag's red flame.
> Comrades, remember me.
> The fascists shot my children first,
> they made me stand and see,
> O dip the flag in my heart's blood.
> Comrades, remember me.
> Spain rose up in the morning,
> roused by the bluster of bullets.
>
> Unbreakfasted, the people,
> put the fascists to rout.
> Spain rose up in the morning,
> Spain rose up in the morning,
> Spain rose up in the morning,
> and drove the fascists out.

Lindsay's poems are interesting because they demonstrate the previously noted characteristics of this kind of writing, the use of heroic stock phrases and images of violence, as well as the casual distortions of fact. The legendary role of the churches as arsenals and forts of the Insurgents has been largely disproved; the "counter-revolution" was a Communist myth, since the real counterrevolution in Spain was within the Republic, and it was led and directed by Communists. Lindsay's poems are interesting also because they probably could not have been written by a man who had actually engaged in the fighting. Any bad poet could have written such a line as "Unbreakfasted, the people," or sacrified accuracy for alliteration by referring to the "bluster of bullets," but a man who had actually seen children shot would have been less glib about the occurrence.

It is worth noting that Lindsay and those like him, including writers like John Malcolm Brinnin, Norman Rosten, Erskine Caldwell, Norman Corwin, Sylvia Townsend Warner, Ruth Deacon, or Theodore Kaghan (all of whom appear in such collections as *Salud!* [6] or *The Heart of Spain*),[7] had their counterparts on the other side, most notably Roy Campbell, more recently the darling of American neoconservatives. Campbell, whose claimed experience in the war ought to have taught him to know better, wrote some of the most bloodthirsty poems to come out of this or any other war. *Flowering Rifle*,[8] for example, in addition to asserting the power of prayer to bring down airplanes and capture tanks ("And with our Pater Nosters and Hail Marys / Were liming aeroplanes like tame

[6] Alan Calmer, ed. (New York: International Publishers, 1938).

[7] Alvah Bessie, ed. (New York: Veterans of the Abraham Lincoln Brigade, 1952).

[8] (New York, London, Toronto: Longmans, Green & Co., 1939). A revised version of the poem was included in *Collected Poems* (Chicago: Henry Regnery, 1957).

canaries"),[9] contains lip-smacking descriptions of the painful deaths of the "heathens":

> . . . Blankets and petrol, then,
> And a great fire exploding, while the men
> Rush backward: and the brainyell of the crew
> Locked in and trapped, comes yodelling wildly through,
> While through the flaming reek of molten rubber
> Is heard the crack and hiss of human blubber,
> Which, when at last the whistling flames are dumb,
> For half an hour prolongs the dismal hum.[10]

The same kind of ignorant callousness dominates other instances of propagandist literature. Upton Sinclair is only one of several writers who undertook novels which would show the absolute virtue of the Loyalist cause and the absolute depravity of the Insurgents. The conventions of this kind of novel are simple: the hero is strong, brave, handsome and immortal; the action must be interrupted from time to time so that the author can explain to the moron in the back row the political implications of this action; the hero is able to perform such incredible feats as bagging an aeroplane with a rifle, or standing off an entire column of the Foreign Legion single-handed; the villainy of the bad guys is made clear, since they are priests who connive at the burning of their own churches, or Americans involved in the German-American Bund, or promiscuous debutantes, or corrupt countesses who maintain dungeons passed down in an uninterrupted line from Gothic fiction.[11]

---

[9] *Ibid.*, p. 56.

[10] *Ibid.*, p. 140.

[11] For example, William Rollins, Jr., *The Wall of Men* (New York: Modern Age, 1938); Ralph Bates, *Sirocco and Other Stories* (New York: Random House, 1939). Equally simplistic novels written from an Insurgent point of view include Helen Nicholson (Baroness de Zglinitzki), *The Painted Bed* (Indianapolis: Bobbs-Merrill, 1938); Percy F. Wester-man, *Under Fire in Spain* (Glasgow: Blackie & Son, 1937).

Sinclair's *No Pasarán!* [12] is perhaps an extreme example, but it does serve as a demonstration of the tired devices that mark this kind of fiction. The hero is a poor young man of German descent who is taken up by rich relatives and exposed to a glittering social world. Unlike Dreiser's Clyde Griffith, however, he is eventually disgusted by the glitter and by his relatives, who turn out to be Nazis, and is drawn closer to a Jewish boy named Izzy, a Socialist, whom he has rescued from the brutality of the police. Sinclair takes us to a Bund meeting, where the storm troopers are warming up for a pogrom, and to a most inspirational and healthy social night at the local solidarity club, an affair which is unfortunately broken up by the Bundists. The hero, who has become disgusted with the casual promiscuity of his debutante inamorata, marries the virgin daughter of the lower classes, a paragon poor and ignorant, but sweet and loving. After a brief but ecstatic honeymoon, he is off with Izzy on a ship bound for the battlelines in Spain, a ship which also gives passage, coincidentally, to his Nazi cousin, who is off to join Franco. In a final apocalyptic scene in the trenches, our hero helps to save Madrid, and with his proletarian rifle kills his cousin, who happens to be strafing the trench in which he and Izzy are fighting. Sadly, Izzy is killed, but this gives Rudy the opportunity to rededicate himself to the struggle for liberty. Should the reader have any questions about the location of right and wrong in this short novel, Sinclair frequently takes time out from the action to explain the virtues of freedom, solidarity, and the proletariat, as well as the evils of anti-Semitism, oppression, and the idle rich.

The ludicrous melodramatics and the really startling coincidences are perhaps peculiar to the kind of author who could invent such a character as Lanny Budd. But Sinclair shared

[12] Pasadena, 1937.

with others a tendency to romanticize war beyond all recognition. The men who fought in Spain, and even those who merely observed the action at fairly close range, had no illusions about the pain of bullets, the hardships of trench warfare, or the reality of death. Sinclair and such other writers as William Rollins, Jr., Percy Westerman, Theodore Kaghan, or a dozen others, lacking the experience of war, lacked also the will or the ability to project themselves imaginatively into violent action, and were therefore unable or unwilling to deal with it realistically. What they produced might be temporarily exciting to the emotions, although even this is doubtful, but it could have little permanent effect. Long before 1936, the romantic view of modern war had been thoroughly debunked, often by the same men who now undertook to prove that the war in Spain was somehow exceptional, and the more explicit examples of propaganda became more rare as the war went on.

But tales of unrealistic heroism on your own side and evil deeds on the other are not the only means by which literature can be used to elicit sympathy and support for a cause, and not a few writers managed to be more realistic about war than either Lindsay or Sinclair without departing from stereotypes of good and evil. Men who had actually seen the war and participated in it could write books which were at once realistic in their descriptions of actual events and blatant appeals for the reader's sympathy for a particular point of view.

Ralph Bates, an English novelist who had been familiar with Spain during the early thirties, had before the war written a realistic and moving novel about life in a small Spanish village during the months immediately preceding the Asturian miners' revolt in 1934. In this novel, *The Olive Field*,[13] it is perfectly clear that the author's sympathies are with the oppressed peasants; the revolt in Asturias has no genuine con-

[13] (New York: E. P. Dutton, 1936.)

nection with the action of the novel, and is brought in to make a political point. Nevertheless, the characters have a life of their own, and seem to be more than the author's puppets. After the war had begun, however, Bates wrote a number of stories for journals as dissimilar as *Esquire* and *Left Review* while serving as a commissar in the International Brigades, and these stories are uniformly pointless and superficial.[14] A typical story of this period deals with a small village near Madrid, recounting a series of incidents occurring in the town, incidents which share only location and the theme that peasants on the Loyalist side are uniformly brave, simple, and dedicated to their cause.[15] The characters have no genuine existence, and Bates seems to have lost the feeling for Spanish peasant life which he manifested in *The Olive Field*.

John Sommerfield, another Englishman, demonstrates a different means of combining realistic description with slanted commentary. Sommerfield was a young Communist who was among the first to join the International Brigades. He fought in the defense of Madrid in the fall of 1936 and returned to England in time to write and publish his memoir, *Volunteer in Spain*, early in 1937. His visit to Spain was brief. The book deals for the most part with the experiences of the Britons and Americans who actually participated in the fighting. *Volunteer* begins with a brief narrative of the author's trip to Spain, by way of the recruiting office in Paris. In the early pages he conveys a good deal of the excitement of those days, of the tensions and enthusiasms of young men going off to save the world. Many of them, like Sommerfield himself, were Communists, and they had the sudden sense that history was moving their world with increasing rapidity toward the dawn of a better Marxian day and that they had been chosen to partici-

[14] *Sirocco and Other Stories.*
[15] "In the Midst of Death We Live," *Esquire*, X, 4 (October, 1938), 64–65, 158–60.

pate in climactic events. This sense first appears in the book when Sommerfield and his British friends arrive at the Quai d'Orsay station to entrain for the Spanish frontier, and find that they are being joined by volunteers from other countries: "We stared at one another, puzzled, delighted, not quite understanding, but full of hope. Under this echoing roof, before the staring electric clock-face, a moment of history was creating itself, of which we, sharing in it, began to be obscurely conscious." (p. 6)

There are other joys in going off to save the world. The ocean trip to Alicante is unpleasant, but once ashore in Spain the volunteers find new wonders: they see a Russian-built truck, and it is "a good lorry, tremendously strong, built sensibly." (p. 54) They receive rifles, they hear a speech by the lengendary Frenchman André Marty, who gained living sainthood in the Communist party by his accidental presence in Sevastopol during the Russian Revolution (p. 41), and they are overjoyed to hear Spaniards shout "Viva Rusia" at them on the assumption that all help from abroad comes from the Soviet Union. (p. 53) It is all made to seem wonderful and inspiring.

Combat is not so romantic. Sommerfield was among the men who were shipped, with very little training, to the defense of Madrid, and much of his description of warfare is realistic. He is most successful in *Volunteer* when he is simply reporting events or recalling what the men felt during the long waits between engagements or during the quiet nights along the front. (pp. 116–21) At one point he provides a moving commentary on war's degradation:

Here I lay, grovelling in a glorified ditch and gnawing at pieces of earthy tinned meat between shell-bursts, listening tensely to the howling in the air that would tell me that one was coming our way, flattening myself against the ground with arms folded over head, waiting for the

explosion and the hail of stones and shrapnel overhead, and then taking
another bite of the meat. And the sun was down and the cold night
coming, and there was only an angry exhausted numbness in my
mind, and a despairing craving for sleep and warmth. And every time
I ducked and covered my head I felt degraded. (pp. 114–15)

Such a passage helps to fulfill Sommerfield's promise to
present a hard, realistic picture of the war. Other passages,
however, reflect a tendency to slip from realistic detail into
impressionistic pseudo-poetic descriptions of bombing planes,
shellings, and rifle fire, which are strangely out of key with
the realism. These descriptions appear in a chapter labeled
"Natural History of the War," a title which demonstrates that
Sommerfield had read Hemingway. The chapter itself shows
that his reading had not taught him much:

Also we learned to know our own bullets' song of flight; we fired
volleys into the night and while the echoes were fading among the hills
we heard a rushing, dying sigh, a disembodied sobbing, and infinitely
melancholy complaint of pierced and wounded air, like the mournful
cry of birds leaving in the night, like the single prolonged beat of
a thousand wings. (p. 99)

Such flights intrude into the narrative pattern of *Volunteer*,
tending to dim the harsh outlines of the battle scenes and
consequently softening and glossing over the grimness of war.

The same effect is achieved by the frequent references in
Volunteer to Sommerfield's political beliefs. Almost every
event is given a dogmatic, ideological interpretation. The people on the Loyalist side are seen in a false light. When a poster
evokes the memory of some militia girls he had seen in Spain,
Sommerfield says of them:

. . . *They* were truly worth remembering, the living symbols of a
whole generation of women who were freeing themselves from the
bondage of centuries, from a triple burden of exploitation, religious,
economic and sexual. A mute submissiveness still lingered in their

large dark eyes, but the bullets in their cartridge-belts were to be directed against the defenders of their tradition. (p. 25)

Whenever the author comments on what he has seen in Spain, the result is passages like this, with the stock phrases ("bondage of centuries," "burden of exploitation," "living symbols of a whole generation,") and its stock interpretation of Marxist-Stalinist doctrine: these girls are evidently unaware of the historical importance of their actions, but this hardly matters, since they have been selected by history to help usher in a new era. Seeing women as symbols relieves the observer of the need to see them as individuals, to see whether the "mute submissiveness" in their eyes is not really disgust at having to take part in men's bloody games, or to discover how they like being pawns of history. Evasions of this same kind keep us from knowing much about the men in Sommerfield's company. They are referred to almost always by their first names (Freddie, Mac, Bill, John, etc.) and few of them are revealed as individuals. When one is singled out, it is as a symbol of the kind of man history (or Communism) can find a use for, like Freddie, the tough, who had "drunk and womanized and fought for the greater part of his life with a cheerful and charming irresponsibility," but who in this kind of situation "was grand." (p. 64) War and the Communist party had made a man of him.

The jargon we have already seen in Sommerfield's description of the militia girls recurs throughout *Volunteer*. One of the most curious manifestations is a patent imitation of the famous discussion of heroic words in *A Farewell to Arms*:

I don't know about heroism, I don't know about the history-book stuff; when you are in a war the orator's phrases and the newspaper words don't mean a thing; expressions like "brave," "victorious," "gallant," become nauseous and shameful. Instead their meaning is transferred to certain places (so that when I spoke of young Simonie having been

at Irun it meant everything) and to things that evoke the memory of
certain scenes. And that song, the unforgettable voices and expressions
of those men, the exhausted gestures of their limbs and bodies, the
lines and composition of the shivering groups that they formed, conveyed in an instantaneous impression the whole of the "heroism," the
whole bones and guts of the Spanish people's struggle. (pp. 74–75)

Sommerfield, after noisily renouncing the use of abstractions
for describing war, immediately falls back on such more modern clichés as "guts" and such phrases as "the Spanish people's
struggle." Time and again Sommerfield deadens the narrative
with similar injections of catch phrases and cant.

Sommerfield's problem is by no means unique. We find it
also in such poets as John Cornford, Tom Wintringham, and
Edwin Rolfe, and in some of the work of Ernest Hemingway.
The writer is exposed to violence and sudden death, and he
feels that he must report these experiences; at the same time
he believes that the war is not only necessary but just, and
that his book must show this. The result is clearly illustrated
in the closing scenes of *Volunteer*. The narrative closes with a
description of the men in Sommerfield's group; in a ravaged
town behind the lines, they stand on a street where two dead
Fascist soldiers lie. The brains of one of the dead men have
spilled into the street, and a dog licks at the mess. A guard
shoots the lean animal and then apologizes to the watching
men: " 'It has to be done. They get the taste for human flesh. It
is bad. . . .' " His explanation is accepted and he returns to
his post. Sommerfield concludes the narrative:

And we stood there waiting, steel-helmeted, hung about with arms
and ammunition, gas-masks dangling on our chests . . . ; and the
rain came down, the broken water-main gushed continuously, the tall
buildings gaped their wounds, and from the corpse in the street the
blood and brains washed slowly away, mingling with those of the dead
dog.
    It was as good a war picture as I could think of. (pp. 151–52)

This is a memorable evocation of the futility and degradation of war, and a powerful metaphor of the bestiality and blood lust which accompany it.

To end on this note, however, would be bad politics, and so Sommerfield appends a chapter in which he repudiates his own metaphor. In his "Final Note," he refers to the event just described as a "sterile horror," and tries to show why that horror is not the important truth about Spain. Unfortunately for his purpose, he has nothing to set against his powerful image but a set of tired abstractions, justifying participation in this war (it is always *this* war) as an effective means of obtaining peace. Because this was an era of peace marches, the Oxford Pledge, and No-More-War, some kind of special pleading is necessary. The argument, however, is based upon such lame phrases as "hatred of war," "there are things worth fighting for and things that must be fought against," "pure pacifism leads to sterility and in times of crisis to the abandonment of effective struggle against war," and references to "peace-loving people." (p. 153) These phrases and their obvious aim show Sommerfield's awareness of the kind of debate that was going on among British intellectuals, but they lose their meaning when juxtaposed against the vivid image of the dead dog and the soldiers.

Civilians who had been caught in Spain by the outbreak of fighting, or who had gone there soon after, also managed to produce books about their experiences before the war was very old. Elliott Paul, who has since made a very good thing out of recapturing and sentimentalizing the past, tried his wings with *The Life and Death of a Spanish Town*,[16] which is in many ways the most innocent of all Spanish Civil War memoirs. Out of an experience which in fact amounted to a

[16] (New York: Random House, 1937.) References here are to the Modern Library Edition, New York, 1942. Page references will be incorporated in the text.

defeat for the Loyalists, Paul constructs a hymn of praise to the Spanish people and to what he regards as their simplicity, their courage, and their belief in liberty and democracy. He mourns for a town captured by the Insurgents, but he shows no real awareness of the fate of such a town, nor of the reality of the struggle going on around him. Despite a fine assortment of ringing words and references to bloodshed, this is a most unwarlike book.

Paul's innocence seems to result from a combination of ignorance and sentimentality. His whole experience of the war was limited to a few months on the island of Ibiza, smallest of the Balearics, months when the only violence on the island consisted of a few scattered bombings and a nearly bloodless invasion. He speaks as an old hand at politics, but actually he knows next to nothing about Spanish political life. Furthermore, Paul seems never to have questioned his emotional attachment to the people of Ibiza. He had lived with them, drunk wine with them, eaten their food, and found them charming, in a primitive way; he was not objective enough to subject them or his own emotions to any intellectual analysis.

Paul's approach results in an emotional, simple-minded book; ironically enough, it at one time enjoyed considerable popularity in this country. Over a harsh and brutal conflict, Paul was able to throw a cloak of nostalgia. He tried to show that the Spanish people were fundamentally honest, if somewhat simple; that they had a pure love of freedom and democracy, whatever party labels might be hung on them; that the peasants and fishermen were "good guys," easily distinguishable from such "bad guys" as the priests and the rich men.

In the first half of the book, a series of impressionistic tone poems gives the reader a modicum of insight into the lives of the residents of the village of Santa Eulalia, and a clear understanding of the syrupy primitivism which underlies Paul's treatment of them. He was enchanted, as writers so often are, by a people who live by ancient trades, who speak a strange tongue, and who maintain a traditional culture in the midst of a world of machinery, uniformity, and *kitsch*. Portraits of individuals seem intended to show that the town was populated by noble savages; this is especially true in the ecstatic portraits of the town's leaders, the captain of a fishing boat and a tavern-keeper. The former is a Communist, but one who has evidently never heard of Karl Marx (pp. 23–24) and who has learned the lessons of communism from the sea, in some unspecified way. The latter is described as the natural leader of the towns-people, but it is never clear why this should be so: "Good men just naturally stood behind him." (pp. 81–82) Nor is it ever clear why the Ibizans, alone among citizens of the Spanish Republic, should be naïve and ill-educated where political matters are concerned. It seems fair to conclude that in truth they were not, but only appeared so to Paul's uncritical eyes.

The melange of styles in which the book is written helps to coat Paul's subject in a romantic haze. Some of the writing is straightforward enough; in the second half of the book there are narrative passages whose terseness reflects the Hemingway influence. But where Sommerfield, for example, varied his narrative with emotional apostrophes to bombs, airplanes, and shells, Paul is more likely to lapse into a windy verbosity, sometimes combined with such rhetorical devices as the rhetorical question, in flights which show his preoccupation with his own emotions:

Old friends! Beloved island of Ibiza! My chosen town! How can I believe that you are of the past, cut off from me as irrevocably as the legendary days of the Moors, the camps of the Romans, the settle-ments of Carthaginians, Phoenicians, Iberians, all lost in the mirrors of history? You are not all dead, my former comrades. There are dawns in unending series to come, and the rising moon will lift the

identical shape of Ibiza from the darkened sea. Shall I ever find your
equal or your equivalent? Can I survive another transplantation?
Shall I always be saying, "Those were the good days. They have been
destroyed." Or can I keep those scenes a while by re-enacting them,
with a pin on the discs of my brain, until they are worn and emit false
tones and eventually are discarded? (pp. 13–14)

The false tones in writing like this must have been audible as
soon as they were sounded. Paul might be forgiven his mixed
metaphors and his bombast if there were any sign that he was
concerned for the fate of his friends, but all his pity is for
himself.

In the first part of *Spanish Town*, Paul has frequent recourse
to another device for holding the reader's attention, as if,
afraid that his descriptions of the town in days of peace may
be boring, he must allude to the horrors that are to come:

Nineteen thirty-six, take your place in the corridor of bloody years!
Be proud, if you can, of what you have evoked and produced and spilt.
No redder blood has trickled down the rocks, no more innocent victims have been led to the sacrifice. The smell of tripes and incense.
Your shrieks are equal of old echoes, your bones will lie in a layer,
nineteen thirty-six, which is now the top but will shift down gradu-
ally. (p. 78)

Such references to bloody deeds point to the failure of the
second half of the book, which is pure anticlimax. To be sure,
this section does have a narrative framework, the sequence of
events in Santa Eulalia from the days just before the generals'
revolt until Paul's departure three months later. But nothing
of importance ever takes place in Santa Eulalia. Control of
the island changes hands twice, but these changes hardly affect
most of the people. A few men, none of much importance in
the book, are carted off to jail; a few others, equally unknown
to the reader, are shot, usually by accident. Cosmi the tavern-
keeper is apparently something of a hero, but we are told so

little about his actions that we cannot judge. When Paul finally leaves the island aboard a German destroyer, taking with him his family and Cosmi, the reader is no longer surprised that the departure is one more anticlimax, for all its rhetorical inflation:

And of the dead empty city (white flag) and stench of fishes and our orange peel of town life and promise, we counted seventeen good men sailing to safety and the future, and if only our German craft would start and get clear, perhaps there would be a future after all.

Cosmi, smiling and inscrutable, and at last propeller, and swinging, now moving, elastic of distance, and we turned, not to pass Santa Eulalia and Arabie and Cosmi's wife, small son and life's savings and shores and coves of dreams, but the other way.

Uncertain click of stereopticon — and the rushing sea. (pp. 423–24)

Spanish Town is a dull and foolish book when read today. In extenuation of its author, it should be pointed out that one reason for this has less to do with his own emotions or talents than with our own experience of destruction in the last twenty-five years. What seemed bloody and terrible in 1937 is to our jaded eyes only a minor incident. Paul regards the bombing of civilian towns as horrible and unthinkable, and so it is. But we live in a world in which a single bomb can obliterate an entire city, in which guided missiles can in a few hours or at most days destroy entire nations or the human race. The twenty-five women and children whose deaths Paul found so shocking diminish to insignificance in the total of casualty figures in the great and little wars since 1939. Too much experience has made us callous about the results of violence reported in this way.

If our callousness helps to account for our lukewarm response to *Spanish Town*, however, the book itself is still the chief culprit. Paul was too concerned with himself, too simple-minded in his views of Spain and her problems, too ready with platitudes encased in hyperbole. His attitude toward the war is entirely emotional: his friends are good guys, they were for the Republic, they must therefore be "democrats," since in this loose jargon "good guys" and "democrats" are synonymous. The history of Spain before and during the Civil War belies Paul's implication that these primitives were political innocents. Such a view had a wide currency outside Spain in the early months of the Civil War, chiefly because it helped to counteract Nationalist charges that all Republicans were *ipso facto* Communists, but it had no basis in fact. If the Ibizans seemed politically inactive, Paul had only to look across the straits to Catalonia, stronghold of the largest and most fervent Anarchist movement in modern history, and politically one of the most militant cities anywhere, to see the fierce and specific political beliefs held by Spaniards.

Paul's book does not share with Sommerfield's an innocent and naïve belief in the automatic triumph of virtue which is ironic in view of the total defeat suffered in Spain by those whom they regarded as virtuous, but both books take too little notice of the true political nature of the Spanish Civil War. Paul writes from the point of view of an aging derelict made homeless by the war, while Sommerfield speaks with the voice of youth, typifying at least one group of the intellectual, idealistic, enthusiastic young men who made the difficult journey to Spain. What *Volunteer* does not show is the shattering disillusion that came to many of these men with the realization that the war was lost. In other books, such as Alvah Bessie's *Men in Battle*, or in the poems of Stephen Spender, we shall see that some writers were less likely to be glib about history and about the necessity for sacrifice.

Spanish Town and *Volunteer* were appropriate to the early months of the Spanish Civil War. In 1937 Sommerfield could still believe what his party wished him to: that the deaths of his friends would be justified by the victory of the great cause they fought in. He dedicated his book to John Cornford, the young and shining knight of British Communism who had died at Teruel: "I did not see him dead; I can only remember him alive and laughing, strong, resolute, and reliable . . . the type and symbol of the youth of today whose conscious task it is to change the world. . . ." (p. 155) Most of the members of Sommerfield's generation came eventually to the hard realization that changing the world as they wanted it changed was not so easy as they had imagined, and that the gods they worshipped were no more powerful than other gods. The shock of this realization is still a powerful political force.

Cornford's name reminds us that a number of writers showed little reluctance to use the names of dead martyrs for the cause. A clear example of this is found in the poems of Margot Heinemann. The object of a touching personal lyric, "Heart of the Heartless World," written by Cornford, Miss Heinemann's answering lyric is curiously detached for a young woman writing of a lover. Love is not mentioned; what seem to have been Cornford's chief attractions for Miss Heinemann were his intellect and his will, his ability to "blueprint" the future which to less gifted young men represented no more than "sapphire dreams."[17] "For R.J.C." analyzes with considerable objectivity Cornford's usefulness to the movement:

> When he began, he talked too fast
> To be heard well, and he knew too much.
> He never had, though learned a little at last,
> The sure, sincere and easy touch
> On an audience, and his handsome head
> Charmed no acquiescence: he convinced and led.

If this sounds rather like a producer's comments on a fledgling television announcer, it might perhaps be explained as an

[17] Margot Heinemann, "For R.J.C.," in *Poems for Spain*, pp. 44–45.

attempt on the woman's part to encourage her soldier-lover
and strengthen him for the struggle. But the poem Miss Heinemann wrote on Cornford's death is in some respects even more
chilling. There is some expression of personal grief, but the
loss to the party is made to seem more important; the final
stanzas illustrate:

> If we have said we'd face the dungeon dark
> And gallows grim, and have not meant to face
> The thin time, meals alone, in every eye
> The comfortless kindness of the stranger — then
> We have expected a privileged treatment,
> And were out of luck. Death has many ways
> To get at us; in every loving heart
> In which a comrade dies he strikes his dart.
>
> *All this is not more than we can deal with.*
>
> In our long nights the honest tormentor speaks
> And in our casual conversations:
> "He was so live and young — need he have died,
> Who had the wisest head, who worked so hard,
> Led by his own sheer strength: whom I so loved?"
> Yes, you'd like an army of Sidney Cartons,
> The best world made conveniently by wasters, second
>   rates [*sic*],
> Someone that we could spare,
> And not the way it has to be made,
> By the loss of our best and bravest everywhere.
>
> *All this is not more than we can deal with.*[18]

The personal note, rather forlornly placed at the end of the
question in this final stanza — "whom I so loved" — is touching, but the word "comrade," the use of the editorial "we" and
the hard, grim refrain overwhelm any personal emotion.

[18] Margot Heinemann, "Grieve in a New Way for New Losses," in
Poems for Spain, pp. 45–46.

Margot Heinemann is no very important figure. The literary autobiographies of men like Stephen Spender and John Lehmann, who were very active in British left-wing intellectual circles during this era, do not mention her, and little she has written since has come to public notice. But the attitudes toward Cornford and her party which these poems reflect are important for the insight they give into the left wing movement of the thirties and the way in which that movement, or at least parts of it, regarded the cause as far more important than anything so ephemeral as a personal relationship between human beings.[19]

By the time Cornford had been dead for a little more than a year, Miss Heinemann could write of the dead in the plural as if none of them had ever had a personal importance for her, and to argue that they had died to save the future:

> It was not a few fields they fought to gain,
> But months and maybe years of war.
> Time's on our side: by time we mean
> The heirs of time they thought worth dying for.
>
> This narrow ridge of time their valour won,
> Time for us to unite, time to discover
> This new offensive is your life and mine,
> One nation cannot save the world forever.[20]

Once again, the poetry itself is flat and lifeless, and on occasion, meaningless.[21] More important, it shows that distance from the scene of conflict undoubtedly helped Margot Heine-

[19] Murray Kempton, in *Part of Our Time*, pp. 222–32, has examined an American relation which, in its inception, illustrates the attitudes which seem to have motivated Miss Heinemann.

[20] Margot Heinemann, "This New Offensive," in *Poems for Spain*, pp. 24–25.

[21] For example, the statement that time is "the heirs of time," which is simply meaningless.

mann contain her emotions, as it did with Lindsay and a good
many other writers. They could write poems and plays which
never questioned the justice of the war or regarded the ravages
of war as anything but the fault of the enemy, because they
regarded the war as an abstraction, a force loosed by history
to demolish fascism. Sommerfield managed to escape with his
preconceptions unchanged, and Paul saw too little of the war
to be very much affected by its destruction. The rapidity with
which an individual writer could change his attitude toward
the war, after exposure to it, is demonstrated by W. H. Auden.
His poem, with its simple title "Spain," is probably the best
known single poem occasioned by the war.[22]

"Spain" was written before Auden's 1937 visit to Spain,
and it remained the only poem he wrote about the war. No
reason has ever been given for Auden's sudden loss of interest
in the Spanish conflict, but we have Stephen Spender's testimony that his single visit to the war was very brief: "He had
offered his services in Spain as a stretcher bearer in an ambulance unit. Yet he returned after a very short visit of which
he never spoke."[23] The poem he wrote before the mysterious
trip is accomplished but doctrinaire.

In "Spain," Auden sees the Spanish Civil War as a pivotal
point between an ordered and sometimes rational past and a
future in which disinterested investigation, personal love, and
orderly lives may again be possible. This vision determines
the structure of the poem; "Spain" opens with a catalogue of
the past, recalling its triumphs of the mind,

[22] Originally published as a separate volume (New York, 1938).
Page references here are to the version appearing in *Poems for Spain*,
pp. 55–58. Auden now says of the poem: "I dislike it very much and consider the last stanza inexcusably false." (Letter to the author, March 3,
1966.)

[23] Stephen Spender, *World Within World* (New York: Harcourt, Brace,
1951), p. 225.

> . . . yesterday the invention
> Of cartwheels and clocks, the taming of
> Horses. Yesterday the bustling world of the navigators . . .

as well as its irrationalities,

> Yesterday the carving of angels and alarming gargoyles,
> The trial of heretics among the columns of stone,
> Yesterday the theological feuds in the taverns
>   And the miraculous cure at the fountain;
> Yesterday the Sabbath of witches . . . (p. 55)

The opening section, devoted to the past, takes up six stanzas; the last three of these end with the refrain which signals the intrusion of the present:

> But to-day the struggle.

Auden then moves directly to the current situation and presents a dialogue between man and "the life," a kind of Nietzschean life-force, in which the latter denies its own divinity ("Oh, no, I am not the mover; / Not today; not to you") and rebuffs man's demand for miracle, pointing out that the conditions of life are of man's own making: "I am your choice, your decision. Yes, I am Spain." (pp. 56–57) In five succeeding stanzas, Auden turns his attention directly to Spain, "that arid square, that fragment nipped off from hot / Africa, soldered so crudely to inventive Europe . . ." and to the men who have gone there to fight: "They floated over the oceans; / They walked the passes. All presented their lives." The war in Spain is symbolic of and crucial for the choices man must make:

> On that tableland scored by rivers
> Our thoughts have bodies; the menacing shapes of our
>   fever
> Are precise and alive. (p. 57)

The possibilities of the future are then explored briefly, but the two final stanzas of this section again end with the refrain, "But to-day the struggle." The final stanzas of the poem return the reader to the present, where the future will be determined:

> The stars are dead. The animals will not look.
> We are left alone with our day, and the time is short, and
>   History to the defeated
> May say Alas but cannot help or pardon. (p. 58)

Auden is most successful in this poem in his half-ironic treatment of the past and his romantic evocation of the future. In viewing the past he neatly juxtaposes the religious arts against religious persecution, and his admiration for the order of classical Greece with the Dionysian "adoration of madmen." In the future, he says, men can look forward to the pleasures which come only with an ordered and settled society:

> To-morrow the rediscovery of romantic love,
> The photographing of ravens; all the fun under
>   Liberty's masterful shadow;
> To-morrow the hour of the pageant-master and the musician,
>
> The beautiful roar of the chorus under the dome;
> To-morrow the exchanging of tips on the breeding of terriers,
>   The eager election of chairmen
> By the sudden forest of hands. (p. 58)

The poet is less successful in his delineation of the present in the crucial middle section, partly because Auden fell victim to his own rhetoric in using so frequently the somewhat melodramatic refrain, "But to-day the struggle," and in such improbabilities as the image of friendship blossoming "into a people's army." More important is the fact that while Auden was able to imagine the past and future he presents, he had so little familiarity with the struggle he was memorializing that he was unable to realize it verbally in any effective way. George

Orwell regarded "Spain" as "one of the few decent things that have been written about the Spanish war," but he went on to point out the weakness of such stanzas as this:

> To-day the deliberate increase in the chances of death,
> The conscious acceptance of guilt in the necessary murder;
> To-day the expending of powers
> On the flat ephemeral pamphlet and the boring meeting. (p. 58)

Orwell takes the second line of this stanza as a text for a sermon on the ills that beset British left-wing intellectuals during the thirties. Such a line, he says, "could only be written by a person to whom murder is at most a *word*." The reality of murder is such as to discourage flippancy in discussing it, but men like Auden knew nothing of that reality: "Mr. Auden's brand of amoralism is only possible if you are the kind of person who is always somewhere else when the trigger is pulled. So much of left-wing thought is a kind of playing with fire by people who don't even know that fire is hot."[24]

[24] George Orwell, "Inside the Whale," in *Such, Such Were the Joys* (New York: Harcourt, Brace, 1952), pp. 184–85.

3. The Bright Cruel Explosion of Hope

THE QUESTION of acquiescence, or even participation, in the "necessary murder" recurs in connection with some of Ernest Hemingway's early writings about the Spanish Civil War, especially his only play, *The Fifth Column*.[25] Hemingway differs from the other writers discussed in the preceding chapter in several ways. For one thing, he knew Spain very well, having gone there first on the urging of Gertrude Stein in 1922, and having returned often. The fishing trip and the festival in Pamplona portrayed in his first novel, *The Sun Also Rises*, give evidence of his love of Spain and his fascination with the customs of her people. Furthermore, he knew war. He had served, and been severely wounded, in the first world war, and in the years between 1919 and 1936 he had made a specialty of violence, as a war correspondent, a hunter, and an aficionado of the bull ring. Finally, when he wrote *The Fifth Column* he had already seen more of the Spanish Civil War than had any of the others so far discussed, with the possible exception of Sommerfield.

[25] Published in *The Fifth Column and the First Forty-Nine Stories* (New York: Charles Scribner's Sons, 1938).

Hemingway wrote a great deal about the Spanish War: a raft of newspaper dispatches, dozens of magazine articles, several short stories, the narration for a moving picture, a play, and his longest novel. Some of this mass of material will undoubtedly be read as long as any of the literature of this war survives. Most of it, unfortunately, was obviously written hastily and carelessly, and too much is patently propaganda. During the war, Hemingway's judgment of the events in Spain was something less than Olympian.

Hemingway was in the United States when the rebellion broke out, and although he did not get to Spain until the following spring, his commitment to the Loyalist cause was clear from the beginning in his use of personal notes to get funds for the government, and his acceptance, in January, 1937, of the chairmanship of the Ambulance Committee, Medical Bureau, American Friends of Spanish Democracy.[26] On his first trip to Spain during the war he wrote the script for the motion picture *The Spanish Earth* and helped in the filming of the picture. He returned to the United States for a short visit, during which he addressed the American Writers' Congress, but in August, 1937, he entered Spain again for a period of almost six months. The major literary fruits of this second visit were *The Fifth Column* and a series of dispatches to the magazine *Ken*. During his third and final visit to Spain he witnessed the departure of the foreign volunteers who had made up the International Brigades.

The exact nature of Hemingway's interest in the war has been the subject of a good deal of critical controversy, stemming chiefly from the question of whether he took the Loyalists' part because of his love for Spain or because he agreed with them politically. For a number of years it was almost a

[26] Carlos Baker, *Hemingway: The Writer as Artist* (Princeton, N.J.: Princeton University Press, 1952), p. 229.

cliché of American criticism that Hemingway's writings during the late thirties had become increasingly political as he awakened to the crisis of his time. Maxwell Geismar, for example, thought that Hemingway was clearly developing politically,[27] while Edmund Wilson, in "Hemingway: Gauge of Morale," spoke of his "Stalinism," and *Time* once spoke of his having had a case of "Marxist measles."[28]

Carlos Baker has more recently attempted to deny that Hemingway's commitment to the Spanish Loyalists was in any narrow sense political. He is able to quote Hemingway himself to the effect that "I had no party but a deep interest in and love for the Republic . . ." (p. 228) as evidence of the absence of any special sympathy for the Communist party in Spain, and Baker explains that "As an artist and man, he was anti-fascist, and had been for years." (p. 224) It is Baker's thesis that Hemingway's interest in Spain was nonpolitical, that it was based on his continuing and consuming interest in art and on his belief that fascism was the only system of government under which a writer could not be rewarded. He was, therefore, simply anti-Fascist; this did not mean, according to Baker, "that, *as an artist,* he was pro-Republican or pro-Communist." (pp. 223–24)

Baker is here evidently reacting to the vociferous anticommunism of our time, and to the widely accepted legend that anyone who sympathized with or aided the Republicans was at the very least a fellow-traveler. Baker's zeal leads him to overstate the case with unfortunate consequences for his criticism. Among other things, he denies that *The Fifth Column* is in any sense propaganda, since Hemingway could hardly have written propaganda if he was not, as an artist, pro-Republican.

[27] *Writers in Crisis: The American Novel Between Two Wars* (Boston: Houghton Mifflin, 1942), p. 80.

[28] Baker, *Hemingway: The Writer as Artist,* p. 237. Subsequent references incorporated in the text.

(p. 234) The truth seems to be that Hemingway was neither a Communist nor a student of Marx, but he admired the way the Communists managed as much as they could control of the war in Spain, he accepted with little question the political tutelage of *Izvestia*'s correspondent in Madrid, and in practice he was a partisan of the Popular Front government and its attitude toward the prosecution of the war. Our own impassioned zealots of anticommunism would probably feel that these facts make Hemingway a dupe or a "comsymp." But this is silly. What Hemingway's views and his own comments upon them show most clearly is that his years of assiduously avoiding politics had left him unprepared for coping with a situation as complex as that in Spain.

Hemingway's initial response to the war in Spain was to express an enthusiasm for the Loyalist cause as great as that of Lindsay or Sommerfield. *The Fifth Column* was written under fire in Madrid in the fall and winter of 1937, and Hemingway commented that while circumstances had delayed its production, he thought "it read well, no matter how it might play. . . ."[29] Hemingway resembled almost everyone else in not having seen the play staged (except for a brief New York run it remained unplayed until a reasonably successful television performance in 1960), but he was almost alone in thinking that it reads well. Edgar Johnson, to be sure, found in the play "not only a new vitality but a high-spirited sense of fun in the midst of seriousness that Hemingway had all but lost since *The Torrents of Spring*"[30] but this was hardly typical of critical response.

However great may have been the strain and exhilaration of writing while the bombs fell, it is difficult to forgive Hemingway for the excesses of *The Fifth Column*. The play reads like

[29] Ernest Hemingway, Introduction to *The Fifth Column*, p. v.
[30] Edgar Johnson, "Farewell the Separate Peace," *Sewanee Review*, XLVIII (July–September, 1940).

the outpouring of a very romantic and very young writer fallen in love with his first lost cause; nothing in Hemingway's earlier work prepares us for this. *The Fifth Column* abounds in picturesque characters: Philip Rawlings himself, the correspondent turned secret agent "for the duration"; the lovely girl with beautiful legs but lamentably bourgeois attitudes (her name, Hemingway writes, "Might also have been Nostalgia"); [31] the little hotel manager, whose quaintness and cupidity Edgar Johnson found highly comic; even, God help us, a Moorish tart with a burlesque-humor accent and a heart of gold. The play is full of windy sentimentalizing of a kind that Hemingway himself had taught us to mistrust, the mouthing of praise for bravery and abstract ideals. More disturbing, *The Fifth Column* contains a different kind of sentimentalizing, a stoic posturing in the face of danger or hardship which almost parodies such earlier Hemingway heroes as Jake Barnes and Frederic Henry.

The Fifth Column is chiefly concerned with Philip Rawlings, ostensibly a newspaper correspondent but actually a counter-espionage agent for the Loyalists, apparently operating under the orders of the OGPU. The main plot is devoted to the affair between Rawlings and the American girl Dorothy Bridges, a Vassar graduate doing a series of magazine articles on the war. The theme of a great deal of the literature of the Spanish War is the conflict between ideology and violence, but in this play the conflict is between ideology and sex, between Rawlings' commitment to the continuing struggle, of which the Civil War is only an episode, and Dorothy's bed. Since in this struggle, violence is allied with ideology, the outcome is never in doubt. Indeed, since Dorothy is one of the least sympathetic of Hemingway's women, only a Hemingway hero would find any grounds for a struggle here at all. Conveniently, the pres-

[31] Introduction, p. v. Subsequent references incorporated in the text.

ence at the end of the play of Anita, the Moorish tart-with-the-heart-of-gold, gives assurance that the triumph of ideology doesn't necessitate even the temporary renunciation of sex.

Rawlings proclaims nostalgia for his former life. We learn that he had been recruited from a useless life into the movement in Cuba and that while he finds certain aspects of his work unpleasant, he is fully committed, realizing that "we are in for fifty years of undeclared wars, and I've signed up for the duration." (p. 95) He evidently misses, however, such amenities of his former life as the proverbial wine, women, and song, and the reasons for his commitment to the cause are not very clear. We are left in doubt whether the desire to help his fellowmen is really more important for Rawlings than the chance at what Edmund Wilson, commenting on this play, called "the headiest of human sports . . . the bagging of human beings." Rawlings himself is unsure about his own motives; when asked by a superior how he got into counterespionage, he answers:

Oh, people started trusting me that should have known better. And I suppose because they should have known better I started getting, you know, trustworthy. You know, not elaborately, just sort of modestly trustworthy. And then they trust you a little more and you do it all right. And then you know, you get to believing in it. Finally I guess you get to liking it. I have sort of a feeling I don't explain it very well. (p. 44)

The trouble with this explanation stems from the vagueness of the word "it." Does "it" refer only to the chance for violent action, "the bagging of human beings," or is "it" an ideology in which Rawlings truly believes? The question is never answered.

No one says of Rawlings what Karkov says of Robert Jordan in *For Whom the Bell Tolls*, that his political development is slight. That is must be, however, is clear not only in the fact that he can be tempted by a woman, herself developed far more physically than politically, but in the very simplicity of the appeal made to him by his friend and colleague, Max, who tells him, "You do it so *every one* will have a good breakfast like that. You do it so *no one* will ever be hungry. You do it so men will not have to fear ill health or old age; so they can live and work in dignity and not as slaves." (p. 79) Even granting that such a speech might have had some impact twenty-five years ago, it is hardly what one hardened activist would have urged on another.

Whatever the nature of his bond, Rawlings is certainly active in counterespionage. In the course of the play he arranges traps for Fascist agents, helps question prisoners and suspected traitors, and helps to carry out a dangerous mission behind enemy lines which leads to the capture of three hundred fifth columnists within Madrid. Through it all he has the stoic courage so necessary to the Hemingway hero, despite occasional attacks of what he calls "the horrorous." Unfortunately, he is also improbably sentimental. Pleading for the life of a sentry whose sleeping on duty allowed a Fascist to escape, he says:

And we used to have a President named Lincoln in America, you know, who commuted sentences of sentries to be shot for sleeping. So I think if it's all right with you we'll just sort of commute his sentence. He comes from the Lincoln Battalion you see — and it's an awfully good battalion. It's such a good battalion and it's done such things that it would break your damn heart if I tried to tell you about it. And if I was in it I'd feel decent and proud instead of the way I feel doing what I am. But I'm not, see? I'm a sort of second-rate cop pretending to be a third-rate newspaperman. (p. 41)

Set against the joys of war, represented by the adventurous deeds and the heroic statements, are the joys of peace, represented by Dorothy Bridges. She is, as Rawlings confesses frequently, bad for him. She is so insensitive as to buy a fur cape while in Madrid, for a price which, as Rawlings grimly points out, is equal to about three years' pay for a soldier in the Brigades. She knows nothing about the political realities, although, she tells Rawlings, she would be willing to learn. She is in fact something entirely new in Hemingway's women; she inherits Brett Ashley's promiscuity, without the integrity which finally made Brett decide not to be a bitch. She is simply "vain, empty and useless."[32] As one critic has pointed out, "Hemingway, in *The Fifth Column*, has begun to symbolize the enemy class by wealthy and unsatisfied American women as he previously ascribed all sexual perversions and incapacities to the rich in *To Have and Have Not*."[33] Among other things Dorothy commits the crime of entertaining Rawlings at the wrong time, so that a young soldier is needlessly killed.

Given these two characters, there cannot really be much suspense in the play, so Hemingway has tried to disguise the thinness of his plot by enlivening the action with violence and humor. In addition to the foray behind enemy lines and the shooting of a soldier on stage, there is shelling going on in the background most of the time, and the characters talk continuously about violence and death. All the violence is, of course, natural to the setting, and it adds a certain excitement to the play. The humor is less successful. Unique in Hemingway's writings, it arises out of the accents of the hotel manager and the whore, and the manager's diligence in sponging food from his guests.

The humorous elements in *The Fifth Column* warrant some attention, because they show the insensitivity characteristic of

[32] Theodore Bardacke, "Hemingway's Women," in John K. M. McCaffery, ed., *Ernest Hemingway: The Man and His Work* (Cleveland, Ohio: World Publishing Co., 1950), p. 349.

[33] *Ibid.*

this kind of writing. And Hemingway, in *The Fifth Column*, has become insensitive, however glibly his characters may talk of the necessity for saving children and dogs from pain and of being kind whenever possible. The attempted humor in the play comes chiefly from wisecracks: "MANAGER: 'Excuse please if disturbation—'; PHILIP: 'Keep it clean you know. There's ladies present.'" (p. 92) made at the expense of these quaint characters; or from their mangling of the English language: "ANITA: 'Hokay. Beautiful? What you want with beautiful when you're through? I know you. Friendly? Hokay; is friendly can be unfriendly. Charming? Yes. Is a charming like the snake with rabbits. Innocent? You make me laugh. Ha, ha, ha. Is a innocent until a prove the guilty." (p. 51) The other "funny" incidents are no improvement: a description of Rawlings' baptizing people in a bar, using a spittoon, or his failure, after a hard night of drinking, to remember that he had moved in with Dorothy, evicting her former lover.

The Fifth Column is shockingly insensitive because it is the work of an artist of whom better things were expected, and who was thought to know better. By no means as inept as *No Pasarán!* or some of the poetry we have been considering, it does share with the rest of this literature which can be called propaganda an oversimplification of the war and the people involved in it. The works discussed in the last chapter and this are very different; Lindsay's poems are deliberate exercises in polemic so exaggerated as to approach caricature, as is Sinclair's novel; Sommerfield's book shows that while war is hell it is also good manly adventure for the best of all causes; Hemingway shows much of the same thing, but the hell has been reduced to the reluctant surrender of an enjoyable bed-partner, and the adventure is even more enjoyable; Paul is filled to overflowing with sentiment. In presenting these apparently different impressions, however, the authors share the common aim of stirring up sympathy and admiration for the Loyalist cause. They also rely on similar conventions: the figures identified with the Loyalists are brave and kind, and certain that the cause is worth any sacrifice — although it might be noted that the supreme sacrifices are seldom made by the authors or their particular heroes. The Fascists are always cruel and selfish, almost always readily identifiable as villains in the milieu of left-wing propaganda during the thirties: army officers, Nazis, absentee landowners, prelates of rich churches in poor areas, "capitalists."

All of this is, of course, essentially unrealistic. Whatever authenticity these authors may have sought to attain by descriptions of persons or locales or bloody action, the reader distant in time cannot accept the oversimplifications upon which their interpretations rest. Simple reason tells us that the primitives of Paul, the poetry-evoking bombardments of Sommerfield, the glib jargon of Lindsay are inaccurate representations of what went on in Spain, and history confirms our doubts — as some of these writers were later to realize. The war was much crueler, dirtier, and duller than it appears in any of these works. Men are not so simply heroic or villainous as those depicted here, nor causes so good or so evil.

None of the writers discussed so far came to grips, in these works, with the problem which was to dominate the literature of the Spanish Civil War, the conflict which arose when ideals were put to the test of violence. Sommerfield has a glimmering, but he shies away from the problem; lest we be discouraged by the image of a frightened man crouching in the mud, we are distracted by an apostrophe to the beauty of shellfire; lest we read too much into the image of the dog and the dead soldier, we are presented with rhetoric about the cause. Hemingway was later to wrestle with the problem through several short stories and his long novel, and to understand it much

more fully, although he never truly solved it. These works
are products of the first year of the war, a time when it
was still possible to believe that the Loyalists would win,
when there seemed to be some reason to hope that a tide of
resistance to the totalitarianism of Hitler and Mussolini was
rising and that it might prove its strength for the first time
in Spain. Literary propaganda continued throughout the war,
but after late 1937 and early 1938 it was of a different kind.
The reality of war was by that time too well known for the
easy heroics we have been discussing, casualty figures were
too high among both soldiers and civilians, and it had become clear that only something like a miracle could save the
Republic.

This analysis has not been friendly to these works, for two
reasons. First, whether consciously or not, they distorted what
was happening in Spain; consequently, any sympathy they
may have generated for the Loyalist cause was based upon
false premises. Second, their conventions and their manner
nullify any possible claim they might make to literary merit.
In the thirties, it was popular in certain circles to believe that
literature could be a weapon in the class war, but these works
help to show that when a writer tried to impose political
dogma upon his material the result might be a weapon but
it was not literature.

Having said this, it is also necessary to soften our judgment of these men by pointing out that most of the writers
who turned out this kind of material were sincere men who
honestly believed in the Loyalist cause. Some might be hacks
who turned out melodramas or bloodthirsty lyrics on orders
from party higher-ups, but others risked considerably more
than their literary reputations. Sommerfield, after all, was in
the front lines; Ralph Bates, who turned out some weak stories,
was a Loyalist officer; Hemingway frequently risked his life

in Spain. Furthermore, although they oversimplified the issues and personalities, their cause was just. The history of this century might be very different if the Western democracies, whose record in Spain was pusillanimous and stupid, had been swayed by what these men wrote, and had understood more clearly the nature of the enemy. Finally, since our focus is on the men whose sympathies lay with the Loyalists, it ought in fairness be noted that the sympathizers of the Insurgents were no more calm, rational, or balanced in their literary propaganda. Even Jack Lindsay at his worst does not come close to the level of abuse and filthy-minded vilification achieved by Roy Campbell.

Twenty-five years after these books were written, their faults are easy to see. Since we face different problems and different enemies, such endeavors have no urgency for us, and without urgency they are very nearly meaningless. They show, however, the powerful feelings aroused by the war in Spain, and to a certain extent the great hopes which arose with the resistance in Spain to the generals' revolt and with the early determination that for once democracy would not surrender to fascism without a struggle. The disappointment of those hopes has had a more permanent effect on our literature.

4. A Delaying Action

THE FACT of violence is always shocking, especially to those whose only previous experience of it has been vicarious. The generation which grew to maturity during the third and fourth decades of this century knew a good deal about violence at second hand. The massive bloodletting of the first world war had produced a profound revulsion. This response was especially strong in England, which had sacrificed most of a generation on the battlefields, but France and Germany had suffered corresponding losses, as had many of the other European nations, and in the United States intellectuals still took their cues from Europe. Remarque's *All Quiet on the Western Front*, Hemingway's *A Farewell to Arms*, Anderson and Stallings' *What Price Glory*, the poems of Wilfred Owen and Siegfried Sassoon, the novels of Ford Madox Ford—all detailed the horrors of war and determined the response of the younger generation to violence. The younger generation learned its lessons well. During the twenties the activities of nations, whether military or not, were viewed with scorn and suspicion: officialdom, the "establishment," had been responsible for the

first world war, and its members were therefore not to be
trusted, their activities to be ignored if possible.

The horrors of war, though farther removed in time, were
also of importance during the thirties, but with changed em-
phases. With the increasing popularity of Marxism among
intellectuals in Europe and this country, the concomitant interest in the Soviet Union, and such different but related phenomena as the "merchants of death" investigations in the
United States, it seemed clear that the establishment had insti-
gated the war, in part at least, for the greater glory and profit
of the munitions makers and therefore of capitalism. Considerable concern about the horrors of war continued to be reflected, in the Peace Pledge activities, the Oxford Group, and
so forth, but a significant number of intellectuals had been
sufficiently influenced by Marxist and Stalinist doctrine to
believe that the characteristic violence of their time would be
revolutionary. If capitalistic wars were wrong, it had to be
recognized that in many nations violence was the only hope
of the proletariat, and that revolutions were a necessary prelude to a new world order.

The writers who went to Spain were mostly of the second
part of the younger generation. They knew that war was terrible, but they also knew that believers in a righteous cause
might sometimes be forced to resort to violence. This attitude
underlies most of the writing discussed in the preceding chapter. But most of those who went to Spain, and even a good
many who did not go, were unable to retain their illusions.
One reason is that, as already noted, the fact of violence is
always shocking. In addition, the violence of the Spanish
Civil War was in certain ways something new. Never before
in the Western world had civilian populations been systemati-
cally bombed as they were in Spain. The airplane was coming
into its own as an instrument of war, and the raining of death

from the skies was especially terrifying. The increased mobility and destructive power of other weapons of war were less spectacular but equally important, because they made clear that modern war was to be waged as much against civilians as against military men. As if the horror of all this destruction were not enough, the writers who paid close attention to the Spanish War, whether or not they were actually fighting in it, began to discover that the issues were not so clear cut as they had believed.

Few of these writers ever changed their fundamental belief that the Spanish Republic was worth saving, but many of them began to question whether its saving was worth the cost. Others noticed that the government of the Republic was not above reproach. Members of the government still played politics, there were still power struggles, the increasing (and eventually decisive) influence of the Communist party bothered a number of people, and the military leadership of the Republican armies was something less than inspired. The last might be accounted for by the fact that almost all high-ranking Spanish officers sided with the Insurgents and that in consequence the Loyalists had to rely heavily on leaders from the Comintern whose metier was more political than military. There were reasons for the other problems, too. But in sum the discovery that the heroes of the Republic had feet of clay, and that the Republic itself was riddled with problems and contradictions, led to disillusion.

The nature and extent of this disillusion varied greatly. Some writers held on as hard as they could to the beliefs which had aroused their interest in Spain; they had varying success. Others simply abandoned belief and surrendered to horror. A few were able to assimilate what they had learned, attempt to understand it, and reorder their views of the world accordingly. The essential difference between these writers and those discussed in the preceding chapters is that for these writers the experience of violence was real and of primary importance. In various ways, as I intend to show, they tried to deal with the problems of ideology and violence.

The line between the simple propagandist and the man who acknowledges the primacy of violence but tries to account for it in ideological terms is not an easy one to draw. The distinction may be clear, however, if we recall Sommerfield's memoir, which is primarily devoted to celebrating the righteousness of the Republican cause and the heroism of its supporters. Whenever Sommerfield lets the mask drop far enough to reveal horrors like those cited in a preceding chapter, he draws it up again immediately; but, in such a poem as Edwin Rolfe's "City of Anguish," the mask slips too far and cannot successfully be replaced, so that the dogma is far less memorable than the experience of destruction. In the first four stanzas of this poem, Rolfe describes an air raid on Madrid from the vantage point of a roof top, the destruction left by the bombs, and the appearance of the city in the light of the following day. The central concern of these stanzas is the senseless destruction of the city and its people:

> All night, all night,
> flared in my city the bright
> cruel explosion of bombs.
> All night, all night
> there, where the soil and stone
> spilled like brains from the sandbag's head,
> the bodiless head lay staring;
> while the anti-aircraft barked,
> barked at the droning plane,
> and the dogs of war, awakened,
> howled at the hidden moon.
> And a star fell, omen of ill,
> and a man fell, lifeless,

and my wife fell, childless,
and, friendless, my friend.
And I stumbled away from them, crying
from eyeless lids, blinded.
Trees became torches
lighting the avenues
where lovers huddled in horror
who would be lovers no longer.[1]

Some of Rolfe's images are fairly conventional: "the dogs of war," and "the bright cruel explosion of bombs." Others are striking, including the image of the sandbag and the neat ironic shift from falling star to fallen man, wife, friend. Rolfe's skill in the poem is further shown in another passage whose rough alliteration is reminiscent of Ezra Pound's experiments with Anglo-Saxon versifications:

Behind you the memory of bomb beats
the blood in the brain's vessels — the dream broken,
sleep pounded to bits by the unending roar of
shell in the air, the silvery bombs descending,
and spit of machine guns and the carnival flare
of fire in the sky.

All of Rolfe's poetic skill goes into the rendering of violence. When he suddenly changes direction in midflight, and turns to a celebration of La Pasionaria, the Communist party's most popular symbol of the new Spain, his invention seems to desert him at once.

After his food
a soldier needs cigarettes, something to read,
something to think about: words to pull
the war-weary brain back to life from forgetfulness:
spirited words, the gestures of Dolores,
majestic Pasionaria, mother of revolutions,
winner of battles, comforter of defenders;

[1] Edwin Rolfe, "City of Anguish," in Alvah Bessie, ed., *The Heart of Spain*, pp. 212–13.

her figure magnificent as any monument
constructed for heroes; her voice a symphony,
consoling, urging, declaiming in prophecy,
her forehead the wide plateaus of her country,
her eyes constant witnesses of her words' truth.

Even if Pasionaria had been the heroine Rolfe makes her out to be, this passage does not fit in the poem. Images of destruction give way in these lines to the vague and honeyed abstractions which were a commonplace of militant left-wing polemic during the thirties, and to an image so imposing as to be inhuman and consequently false. The inappropriateness of this paean of praise is emphasized by Rolfe's return, at the end of the poem, to his earlier manner. In the fifth and final section we are plunged back into the realities of war, and we feel again the special shock that the brave young men of the Spanish Civil War endured when they discovered that, as Orwell put it, "the essential horror of army life . . . is barely affected by the nature of the war you happen to be fighting in."

No man knows war or its meaning who has not
stumbled from tree to tree, desperate for cover,
or dug his face deep in earth, felt the ground
        pulse with
the ear-breaking fall of death. No man knows war
who never has crouched in foxhole, hearing
the bullets an inch from his head, nor the zoom of
planes like a Ferris wheel strafing the trenches . . .

War is your comrade struck dead beside you,
his shared cigarette still alive in your lips.

In "City of Anguish," Rolfe tries to use Pasionaria as a symbol of the ideals which make the war justifiable and therefore bearable. But he is not a good enough poet to accomplish this, and we may suspect that the reason for his failure was the fact that the destruction and chaos he witnessed made a far deeper impression on him than did the heroine. When he came to write the poem, in any case, he was able to render the horror far more vividly than its rationalization.

Time after time, in the work of men who had been made aware of the destructiveness and brutality of the war in Spain, we find a similar rendering of experience, accompanied by the attempts to use political belief as a talisman to keep reality at a distance. Time and again, in the work of many writers, we find that the reality overpowers the ideas. Arthur Koestler's publishers provided an example of this when they combined his harrowing "Dialogue with Death" with a disparate and unconvincing piece of hackwork purporting to give the facts about the war in Spain. As Koestler has since revealed, the more lurid sections of *The Spanish Testament* were the work of a Communist party propagandist in Paris.[2]

Whatever the circumstances of its composition, the first part of this book leaves no lasting impression; rather the record of Koestler's capture and imprisonment, his mental processes while under sentence of death, remain with the reader. Implicit in *The Spanish Testament*, as in so much of the literature of this phase of the war, is the question: Can the war be justified if it causes such hardships? The affirmative answer is far less strong for Rolfe and Koestler than it was for Sommerfield or Lindsay.

More touching and on the whole more successful were the efforts of a young British poet, John Cornford, the golden young man of British Communism during the mid-thirties. As we have already seen, Cornford was the object of Margot Heinemann's concern, and Sommerfield's book was dedicated to his memory. Stephen Spender and John Lehmann were convinced that he was unusually gifted as a poet, and both speculated that if he had survived the Spanish War he might have

[2] Arthur Koestler, *Invisible Writing* (London: Collins; Hamish Hamilton, 1954), pp. 333–35.

solved the problems of making poetry of Communist orthodoxy. The history of English poetry and politics since 1939,
and the very personal note struck in Cornford's most distinctive
poetry, suggest that, contrary to such expectations, Cornford
might have been more likely to follow the route of disillusion
and withdrawal taken by Spender after 1939. In any case, his
poems are far more interesting than the effusions of the propagandists; they give evidence of real talent, and they reflect
the struggle of a sensitive and intelligent young man to reconcile his experience with the vision he had followed to Spain.

Most of Cornford's verse is intended to urge the glories of
the Communist party and to remind the individual of his duty
to act as the party commands him to. His major theme is
self-immolation, which is seen as a necessary concomitant to
commitment. At the same time, his poems are not so much
concerned with urging others to join him in the crusade as
with the necessity for overcoming his own doubts and hesitations. In the poem "Full Moon at Tierz: Before the Storming
of Huesca,"[3] he wills himself to act in the face of danger,
since history no longer allows unlimited time for orderly
progress:

> The past, a glacier, gripped the mountain wall,
> And time was inches, dark was all.
> But here it scales the end of the range,
> The dialectic's point of change,
> Crashes in light and minutes to its fall.

At such a time, the individual must act: "We are the future.
The last fight let us face." The battle which impends is part
of this final fight, and therefore of absolute importance in
determining whether the ideals and ideology of communism
will prevail. In the second section of the poem, Cornford seeks
to draw strength from an invocation of party heroes like

[3] John Cornford, in *Poems for Spain*, pp. 26–28.

Maurice Thorez and Georgi Dimitrov, and from the party's
own program: "Here what the Seventh Congress said, / If
true, if false, is live or dead. . . ."

The pressures on the individual in such a situation are
very strong, and Cornford admits his loneliness and his weakness; for the party or for history there are no hesitations or
doubts, but the individual who serves them cannot be oblivious
to his own problems:

> Though Communism was my waking time,
> Always before the lights of home
> Shone clear and steady and full in view —
> Here, if you fail, there's help for you —
> Now, with my Party, I stand quite alone.
>
> Then let my private battle with my nerves,
> The fear of pain whose pain survives,
> The love that tears me by the roots,
> The loneliness that claws my guts,
> Fuse in the welded front our fight preserves.
>
> Oh, be invincible as the strong sun,
> Hard as the metal of my gun,
> Oh, let the mounting tempo of the train
> Sweep where my footsteps slipped in vain,
> October in the rhythm of its run.

Following a rather obvious structural pattern (the crisis;
its importance; its meaning for the individual; resolution)
Cornford in the final section evokes a vision of the world
whose fate depends on events in Spain:

> Now the same night falls over Germany
> And the impartial beauty of the stars
> Lights from the unfeeling sky
> Oranienburg and freedom's crooked scars.
> We can do nothing to ease that pain
> But prove the agony was not in vain.

England is silent under the same moon,
From Clydeside to the gutted pits of Wales
The innocent mask conceals that soon
Here too our freedom's swaying in the scales.
Oh, understand before too late
Freedom was never held without a fight.

Freedom is an easily spoken word
But facts are stubborn things. Here, too, in Spain
Our fight's not won till the workers of all the world
Stand by our guard on Huesca's plain,
Swear that our dead fought not in vain,
Raise the red flag triumphantly
For Communism and for liberty.

Cornford's poetry has serious failings. He is often awkward when struggling to work in the "correct" names of places and heroes. The regular rhyme pattern, varied occasionally by the approximate rhymes so characteristic of modern poetry (i.e., Aragon-begun-tone; roots-guts; nerves-survives-preserves) shows no special skill or real originality. To make too much of such difficulties, however, would be unfair. Surely it is asking a great deal to demand consummate technical mastery in verse written on battlefields. A more serious problem is Cornford's excessive reliance on the cant words and phrases drawn from Communist discourse: "history" and "freedom" used carelessly, "not in vain." As used here, such words do no more than arouse a sympathetic emotion in the reader, and repetition does not make them any more palatable ("freedom" is invoked four times in the final section, the phrase "not in vain" is used twice). It is impossible, twenty-five years after this poem was written, not to hear the false ring of this rhetoric, or to avoid the conviction that it was largely the unthinking acceptance and use of such terms that doomed most of the political poetry of the thirties to early obscurity.

But Cornford's poetry has important virtues as well as failings. "Full Moon at Tierz," whatever its weaknesses, displays
a fine talent for metaphor. Cornford's use of words sometimes
makes his verse flat, but the metaphors of the glacier as history,
of time present as a "cataract" whose course men must try to
direct, and of history as a train rushing into the future, have
considerable power and originality. The first stanza of the
final section, beginning "Now the same night falls over Germany . . ." is less melodramatic and more powerful than
the similar final stanza of Auden's "Spain." These images
help give the poem the "hard-muscled" quality which attracted
John Lehmann's praise, and they redeem it from the banality
of some of its diction.

There is evidence here that Spender and Lehmann may have
been correct in their assessment of Cornford as an unusually
talented young poet. This is not to say, however, that he would
have developed or helped develop either the proletarian poetry forecast by Christopher Caudwell[4] or the "orthodox communist poetry" anticipated by Spender.[5] As a very young man,
writing under conditions inimical to poetry, Cornford found
it necessary to bolster frail inspiration with cant; as a mature
poet he might well have found that such doctrinal counters
were necessary proofs of orthodoxy but that they would not
serve for poetry.

The older poet might also have found personal emotion a
more enduring subject for poetry than was politics, as Spender
later did. The personal note is struck more strongly in another
of Cornford's Spanish poems, "Heart of the Heartless World."[6]
Evidently meant for Margot Heinemann, the poem uses none
of the political jargon of "Full Moon at Tierz," and the poet

[4] *Illusion and Reality* (New York: International Publishers, 1947),
pp. 270ff.
[5] Stephen Spender, Introduction to *Poems for Spain*, p. 12.
[6] In *Poems for Spain*, p. 21.

is more concerned here with his love for a young woman than
with history and the party:

> Heart of the heartless world,
> Dear heart, the thought of you
> Is the pain at my side,
> The shadow that chills my view.
>
> The wind rises in the evening,
> Reminds that autumn is near.
> I am afraid to lose you,
> I am afraid of my fear.
> On the last mile to Huesca,
> The last fence for our pride,
> Think so kindly, dear, that I
> Sense you at my side.
>
> And if bad luck should lay my strength
> Into the shallow grave,
> Remember all the good you can;
> Don't forget my love.

Such a poem indicates that Cornford was not always capable
of sublimating his own emotions in "the welded front our fight
preserves." His final injunction could have been issued by
any soldier in any war, and it is not untypical of the soldiers
in the Spanish Civil War. The poets far behind the lines or
in far-off countries might steadfastly write as if the war in
Spain were absolutely unique in all particulars, as if the fears
and longings of other wars had no place there. The men who
were fighting the war were not always so sure.

Cornford's poems help to remind us of the realities of the
Spanish Civil War. The men who fought in it, whether or not
they wrote about their experiences, were men like any others.
They had their moments both of fear and of confidence, they
missed familiar faces, they believed in the justice of their
cause. They also suffered and died. Many, like Cornford,

Christopher Caudwell, Ralph Fox, and Charles Donnelly, to name a very few, died young, before the dimensions of their talent or its direction could become clear. Their deaths, and the work they left behind them, help to remind us that the Spanish Civil War was not merely a political struggle or an occasion for the composition of literary gems or dogmatic interpretations of history.

Cornford's poems, in particular, are interesting evidence that even under the stress of battle, an attempt could be made to apply the doctrines of a political ideology to the events in Spain. If Cornford is not so terrorstruck as Edwin Rolfe, he is far from being so glib and facile as John Sommerfield. In "Full Moon at Tierz," violence has begun to make an impression, but it can still be related to abstractions; in "Heart of the Heartless World," the approach of violence seems to have made the consolations of ideology less certain.

"City of Anguish" and "Full Moon at Tierz," and the work of such soldier-poets as Tom Wintringham, Esmond Romilly, and John Lepper, show that men who had actually seen what war was like in Spain still struggled to find explanations in their beliefs. Day Lewis's poems show that civilians could also see both sides of the war, not only the "big picture" emphasized in the newspapers and magazines, but the destruction and its implications for the world. There is an interesting parallel between the poems of Wintringham, a hard-bitten veteran of World War I and of long service in the Communist party, and those of George Barker, one of the most powerful of the generation of British poets which came to prominence during the thirties.

Wintringham's poetry is dominated by the belief that ultimate victory in Spain will bring a new day bright enough to justify the sacrifices made in the war. Occasionally, in such a poem as "The Splint,"[7] Wintringham allows less ideological notions to intrude, but for the most part he saw the war as Armageddon, with himself and his comrades as the ushers of the future:

> Neither fools nor children we who are joining
> (Twenty years ago I knew war's face)
> We make what others wreck into our gaining,
> Into our choice.[8]

> Our enemies can praise death and adore death;
> For us endurance, the sun; and now in this night
> The electric torch, feeble, waning, but close-set,
> Follows the surgeon's fingers; we are allied with
> This light.[9]

Here, in contrast to Rolfe's shock at destruction, we are assured that the destruction will be given meaning. The cause is more important than the personal wound or the private fear; it is worth the sacrifice it exacts.

Wintringham makes this idea even clearer in the poem "Monuments," in which he suggests that all the relics of the war should be piled together: "Shell-splinters from University City," "a false coin stamped in Burgos by a traitor," "earth from the bullring / Where they shot the prisoners in Badajoz," and "earth from Durruti's grave," among other things.[10] Such a collection will be a true memorial to the war and its victims:

> Take then these metals, under the deep sky
> Melt them together; take these pieces of earth

[7] In *Poems for Spain*, p. 95.
[8] "Barcelona Nerves," in *Poems for Spain*, p. 30.
[9] "Granien," in *Poems for Spain*, p. 41.
[10] In *The Heart of Spain*, pp. 455–56. Originally published in *Volunteer for Liberty* (Barcelona, November, 1938). There is an almost painfully obvious irony in the fact that Generalissimo Franco has created such a monument to honor the war dead.

> And mix them; add your bullets,
> And memories of death;
> You have won victory,
> People of Spain,
> And the tower into which your earth is built, and
> Your blood and ours, shall state Spain's
> Unity, happiness, strength; it shall face the breath
> Of the east, of the dawn, of the futures where there will
>   be no more strangers . . .

The difficulty with poems like "Monument" is not so much that the victory they forecast never came, but that they do not convince us that their victory would have been all they said, or that it would indeed have justified the sacrifices. Wintringham's images are more real than those of Jack Lindsay, and he does not shrug off the lessons of war as easily as did Sommerfield, but he is no more successful than they in giving life to his vision of the future. "Unity, happiness, strength" are far too vague when placed against the destruction seen in Rolfe's poems, or when compared to the work of writers like Alvah Bessie, Robert Payne, and Stephen Spender. There is a question here of poetic talent and of the opportunity for exercising it. George Barker, obviously enough, was a more gifted versifier than Tom Wintringham, a more practiced poet than John Cornford. Far from the actual fighting in Spain, Barker had time to develop his imaginative idea of the war and project his vision in words. These are enormous advantages, and it should not surprise us that when Barker gave voice to ideas similar to Wintringham's and Cornford's he should do so more skillfully.

The comparison is probably closest when we put Wintringham's notion of a monument from which the new Spain will arise next to Barker's poetic conception of the spirit of the Spanish people as a Phoenix which will arise out of the ashes of war. Barker's ability to conceive imaginatively a chaotic world undoubtedly stems from his vision of existence and his celebration of chaos as a necessary concomitant of a vigorous and pulsating life. In the special conditions of the Spanish Civil War, ideological considerations led many writers to gloss over the unpleasant facts of destruction; Barker turned those facts to the service of his vision.

In "Elegy for Spain," Barker provides a myriad of images of devastation, but speaks of the eventual triumph of the Loyalist cause as having been made inevitable by the blood shed in the war. The stanzas of dedication "to the photograph of a child killed in an air-raid on Barcelona" express horror at "the crime of the bloody time," but make it clear that the living must accept the challenge of the times: "And if I feel your gaze upon me ever, / I'll wear the robe of blood that love illumines." [11] The recurrent theme of the poem itself is of death as a sacrifice to future greatness and future freedom:

> This flower Freedom needs blood at the roots,
> Its shoots spring from your wounds, and the bomb
> Booming among the ruins of your houses, arouses
> Generation after generation from the grave
> To slave at your side for future liberation.[12]

In "Elegy for Spain," death is acknowledged as a kind of defeat, but not as the end of hope. Death is a condition of the life that must follow. The final stanzas of the poem are an ode to the regeneration of Spain:

> What is there not in the air any longer,
> Stronger than songs or roses, and greater
> Than those who created it, a nation
> Manhandling god for its freedom? Lost,
> Of my ghost, the first fall, but not lost

[11] *Collected Poems of George Barker: 1930–1955* (London: Faber & Faber, 1957), p. 98.
[12] *Ibid.*, p. 100.

The will to liberty which shall have liberty
At the long last.
So close a moment that long open eye,
Fly the flag low, and fold over those hands
Cramped to a gun; gather the child's remains
Staining the wall and cluttering the drains;
Troop down the red to the black and the brown;
Go homeward with tears to water the ground.
All this builds a bigger plinth for glory,
Story on story, on which triumph shall be found.

"Elegy for Spain" shows that the Loyalist defeat did not substantially change Barker's view of the Spanish War. The poem echoes his earlier mentions of Spain, evidently because, like a number of other writers, he regarded the fighting in Spain as only one manifestation of the violence which was wracking the world. This view is clear in the earlier long poem, "Calamiterror," occasioned by the death of Barker's child. In the final canto of "Calamiterror," Barker arrives at a resolution of his grief in the realization that the struggle for life continues, despite the deaths of individuals; and events in the Spanish War inspired that resolution:

Continually the women weeping in Irun's ruins
Call in distress with voices like swans;
I hear that cry which breaks the womb or room
Wherever I stand, and forces me to go.
The swan my world with a myriad at her breast,
The foaming human struggling, I hear their cry;
The feminine weeping and the masculine agony
Meet at the throat and make the swan's song.

Not over the National spoken and not shown at cinema
To blackout Paramount with the facts like light,
The horror facts, the human in its horror derelict,
Wales and Northumberland wastes whose day of dark
Shows better the bare and bony human. How can he cease
From political fight, how can his sword sleep in his hand,

> When a dark time in a dark time
> Inundates and annihilates the mind? [13]

Barker's variation on Blake, the insertion of the word "political," was not sufficient to convince the Communists that his ideas were the right ones. Stephen Spender, then a member of the Communist party, reviewed "Calamiterror" in one of the party's journals and objected that while the poem did show Barker's awareness of the state of the world, it did not reflect a political attitude that could be called "correct or even constructive." [14] Spender acknowledged his admiration for Barker as a poet, but in comparing "Calamiterror" to Rex Warner's *Poems* he observed disparagingly that "Irun's ruins would speak to Warner with the voice of conscience demanding the voice of protest; they become part of Barker's spiritual habitation. . . ." Spender sees this as an objection, but we are not bound to accept his judgment that Barker's poem is deficient in conscience or in protest, or that Warner's more explicit sermonizing is preferable.

Barker's poems of the Spanish Civil War raise problems that we have encountered before in different form. Like Sommerfield, Kaghan, Wintringham, and others, he does not accept destruction as a reason for surrender; on the other hand, he is less facile than Sommerfield, or such other rearguard writers as Norman Rosten and Norman Corwin, avoiding the easy assurance that victory *in this war* is made certain by "Irun's ruins." Barker envisions the world as an arena for continual struggle; if freedom is worth having, it demands sacrifices. Barker might well have had in mind Thomas Jefferson's famous dictum when he wrote "Calamiterror":

God forbid we should ever be 20 years without such a rebellion. . . . What country can preserve its liberties if its rulers are not

[13] *Ibid.*, pp. 58–59.
[14] "New Poetry," *Left Review*, III (July, 1937), 360.

warned from time to time that this people preserve the right of resistance? Let them take arms. The remedy is to set them right as to facts, pardon and pacify them. What signify a few lives lost in a century or two? The tree of liberty must be refreshed from time to time with the blood of patriots and tyrants. It is its natural manure.[15]

Barker's conception of the war was much closer to Jefferson's than to that manifested in Spender's prose. Spender's poetry, as we shall see a little later, is a different matter.

The most lengthy and laborious attempt to salvage some order out of chaos, and the best-known single work on the Spanish War, is Ernest Hemingway's *For Whom the Bell Tolls.*[16] In an earlier chapter, I noted the difficulties Hemingway encountered in *The Fifth Column.* It is to his credit that he did not remain tied to the simplistic interpretation of the war which dominated the play. Throughout the war, from 1937 until the end of the war, and even to the publication of *FWBT* in 1940, Hemingway struggled with the problem of the meaning of the war and the means for expressing his ideas. He wrote more about the Spanish War than any other individual: newspaper dispatches, magazine articles for *Ken,* short stories, a play, a novel. In the articles and dispatches he is not at his best. Most of the time, in the nonfiction, he is frankly a propagandist, defending the Loyalists, using his polemical talents to delineate the Insurgent's perfidy. But in his short stories, published in *Esquire* and *Cosmopolitan* between October, 1938, and October, 1939,[17] he is obviously struggling with

15 Letter to Col. William Smith, 1787.

16 (New York: Charles Scribner's Sons, 1940.) For convenience, the title will be abbreviated *FWBT* in the discussion; page references will be incorporated in the text.

17 These included: "The Denunciation," *Esquire,* X, 5 (November, 1938), 39, 111–14; "The Butterfly and the Tank," *Esquire,* X, 6 (December, 1938), 51, 186, 188, 190; "Night Before Battle," *Esquire,* XI, 2 (February, 1939), 27–29, 91–92, 95, 97; "Nobody Ever Dies," *Cosmopolitan,* CVI (March, 1939), 29–31, 74–76; "Under the Ridge," *Cosmopolitan,* CVII (October, 1939), 34–35, 102–06. None of these stories was

his material, trying to find his way to an artistic rendering of his experience. None of the stories is successful; all suffer from wordiness, pointlessness, and a general lack of precision. But when we consider *The Fifth Column* and these stories, we can see more clearly how far Hemingway had progressed when he came to write *FWBT*.

Many of the devices and attitudes manifested in the stories were discarded when Hemingway came to write his novel. In the stories he made use of a first-person narrator, who is much like the author, very thinly disguised. For the broader canvas of the novel he discarded a "character" who is obtrusive, sentimental, and a poor storyteller. The stories suffer further from a rambling discursiveness which is wholly unsuited to the Hemingway style, and they are blunted by the author's inability to pare away inessential material. *FWBT* is not the most rigidly controlled of his novels, but Hemingway had a more secure grip on his characters than he had shown in these stories.

Hemingway's attitude toward the war and the people engaged in it also underwent considerable change after he had written the five stories. Each of the three *Esquire* stories is disturbingly juvenile in one way or another. "The Butterfly and the Tank" ends with an attempt to turn into tragedy an incident that had been depicted as humorous. "Night Before Battle" is reasonably successful in conveying the atmosphere of a beleaguered city, but it falls flat; what might have been a touching sketch of two men trying to relax in the short rest period between battles is lost in a welter of dull characters and

collected in a book by Hemingway, and when *Esquire* proposed including three stories in a book, Hemingway objected strenuously through his lawyers, first on the ground that he had changed his mind about the Spanish Civil War, later on the ground that he now regarded the stories as unsuccessful fiction.

pointless dialogue. Hemingway is clearly fascinated by the picturesque, and is unable to separate it from the essential.

The worst and the most interesting of the *Esquire* stories is "The Denunciation," which displays the "Hemingway code" and which shows how frivolous that code can be made to look. The narrator is an old habitué of a Madrid bar called Chicotes. One night he sees in the bar another prewar habitué whom he now knows to be a Fascist flyer, and who must therefore be in Madrid as a spy. It is the narrator's duty to turn the man in to the police, but he is reluctant to do so because in the old days he had shot with the man, and had seen him behave with real grace while gambling. The narrator manages to shift the responsibility to an old waiter, who also recognizes the flyer, and after considerable backing and filling and unsuccessful attempts to elicit advice from the narrator, the waiter calls the police. The narrator leaves before they arrive, goes to his hotel, and calls a friend at *Seguridad* with the request that the flyer, before he is shot, be told that he was betrayed not by the waiter but by the narrator. His meditation on this act is instructive:

> All we old clients of Chicotes had a sort of feeling about the place. I knew that was why Delgado had been such a fool as to go back there. He could have done his business some place else. But if he was in Madrid he had to go there. He had been a good client so the waiter had said and we had been friends. So I was glad I had called my friend Pepe at Seguridad headquarters because Luis Delgado was an old client of Chicotes and I did not wish him to be disillusioned or bitter about the waiters there before he died.[18]

This is truly appalling, not only for the fake concern it expresses for Delgado, but for the insensitivity toward the waiter's feeling displayed by the narrator, who is portrayed as a strong believer in the Loyalist cause and in its concern for

[18] "The Denunciation," *Esquire*, X, 5 (November, 1938), 114.

liberty and equality. The narrator decides that the waiter must bear the burden of guilt for turning Delgado in; implicit is the belief that such a man could not possibly have the fine feelings of aristocrats who had shot together before the war. Had Hemingway deliberately set out to write a parody demonstrating the shallowness of the kind of romantic gesture so popular with "code heroes," he could not have demonstrated it more clearly. The story seems at least to have shown Hemingway that this attitude and this method would not serve for portraying the Spanish Civil War, and Robert Jordan is wholly incapable of the narrator's gesture.

In all of these stories Hemingway is clearly struggling to make sense of what he saw. None of the stories is as blatantly propagandistic as *The Fifth Column,* but in the stories he is still attempting to arouse sympathy for his cause. At the same time, he is beginning to be made uncomfortable by the conflicts between his new-found ideology and his old code of grace and honor, and by the contradictions between the publicity picture of the happy, triumphant Spanish people and what he knew of the treason, laziness, and cruelty on the Loyalist side. Hemingway does not play a heroic role in his contemporaries' reports on the Spanish conflict,[19] but *FWBT* shows clearly that he was not unaware of the complexity of the conflict, and in much of his writing from Spain he tries desperately to identify and condemn the people and movements he felt were betraying the Loyalist cause.

The need to dissociate oneself from the undesirable elements was epidemic in Spain, but it hit Hemingway harder

[19] Probably the most revealing story is that told by Josephine Herbst in her memoir, "The Starched Blue Sky of Spain," in *The Noble Savage,* I (March, 1960), 76–117. See page 142. It is clear in Miss Herbst's narrative that Hemingway was far too credulous in accepting what he was told by his friends in the government or those "in the know," a fault which can be ascribed to Robert Jordan of *For Whom the Bell Tolls.*

than most, perhaps because he was at once least sure of himself and most determined not to be hoodwinked. A stranger to political ideology and political warfare, he tried to define his own position by eliminating anything that would not fit into it. He seems to have been reluctant, perhaps wisely, to commit himself to any group or any system of belief, as if such commitment would betray forever the tough-minded independence he valued so highly. He had written, after all, that integrity in a writer is like chastity in a woman, once gone it is irretrievable. In these stories, his struggle to retain his integrity is at least partly responsible for his failure. Unable to use his art simply as propaganda, in the manner of a Paul or a Lindsay, he was yet convinced that the Loyalist cause was just and that defeat for that cause would be tragic. To reconcile his conflicts he tried to write stories which would show his sympathy for the Republic but which would also show that he retained his objective eye and clear head. In the stories he accomplished neither.

His major attempt, however, was in the novel, *FWBT*. This is the most impressive and memorable novel written about the Spanish Civil War, and while not Hemingway's best, it is his most ambitious, most difficult to evaluate, and most interesting. It is his most ambitious because he is working here with a broader canvas than in any of his other novels, attempting to give the book what has been called its epic scope[20] by extending the action beyond the central character to the guerilla band which assists him, to the guerilla band of El Sordo, and beyond that to the headquarters of General Golz and the nerve center of Madrid. It is the most difficult to evaluate because Hemingway succeeds so brilliantly in solving some problems and fails so dismally in solving others. It is the most interesting because of its scope, because of its successes and failures,

[20] Baker, *Hemingway: The Writer as Artist*, pp. 245–50.

and because Hemingway attempts to do so many things he had never done before, things which he never attempted again.

It is worth noting that there is less critical agreement about *FWBT* than about any other Hemingway novel. Carlos Baker, for example, clearly feels that the novel is a modern classic, and that Hemingway successfully hurdled the obstacles in the way of fictional treatment of political matters.[21] Some critics, typified by Maxwell Geismar, saw *FWBT* as a further step (after *To Have and Have Not*) toward "political responsibility," although Geismar noted that Hemingway was not yet the equal of Silone or Malraux as a political novelist. Others, like Edwin Berry Burgum, far from regarding the novel as a manifestation of political responsibility, regarded it as a betrayal of the Spanish people and the Loyalist cause, so flagrant as to be pro-Fascist. Another group has been less interested in what the novel showed about Hemingway's politics than in what is showed about his writing. It has been called everything from a classic to a disaster.

Critics of the novel have called attention to its central problem, a problem deriving from Hemingway's special experience. Most of the writers who dealt with the Spanish Civil War came to Spain with what they thought of as firm political ideals, but with very little knowledge of violence or of how it might affect those ideals. For Hemingway, on the other hand, violence had always been a consuming interest; where others had to face the difficulties of fitting their new knowledge of violence into an ideological framework, with the alternative of abandoning their ideology, Hemingway had to try to change his interpretation of violence to fit his new view of the world. It is a critical cliché that in Hemingway's work before *To Have and Have Not*, violence is simply a condition of life, and a constant threat to the individual. Death or a wound may

---

[21] *Ibid.*, p. 245.

come from the uncontrolled violence of war or from the contained and circumscribed violence of the bull ring, but it is always a present possibility, no farther away than the next hour or the next day. The moral responsibility for violence is not laid at the door of any individuals or group; as one of the conditions of life, violence is not anyone's "fault."

In *To Have and Have Not*, Hemingway shifted away from this view of violence, although not very far away. Harry Morgan, like Jake Barnes or Frederic Henry, is a victim of forces beyond his control, forces which are given at least partial identification. In writing about the Spanish War, Hemingway went a good deal farther. Responsibility for the war and therefore for all of the violence is laid at the door of the Fascists. At the same time, the Loyalists must also engage in violence, and for the first time in Hemingway's writing, bloodshed is given a justification, since the Loyalists' violence is at the service of the people's desire to live in peace and with justice. The shedding of blood has come to involve moral responsibility. A further complication is the idea of duty. Other Hemingway heroes felt a need to act with courage and grace in the face of danger because of a sense of personal honor, imposed from within, or because they were committed to a code of behavior which their sense of personal honor would not permit them to betray.

With Robert Jordan, however, we have for the first time a Hemingway hero who believes that his actions can and will affect the destinies of other men, and who acts with the sense that he is therefore responsible to those others. Given his ideological reasons for joining the Loyalists, Robert Jordan submits to a discipline which is necessary to the successful prosecution of the war and which makes killing a duty. For the first time violence is at the service of Hemingway's vision of a world in which violence need no longer be a condition of life. This is a drastic change, and we have already seen Hemingway's attempts to adjust to it in *The Fifth Column* and the short stories.

Hemingway had to try, in *FWBT*, to show that an ideology he had only partly assimilated justified the violence of the war, and the major problems of the novel arise from this attempt. In the first place, Hemingway had to provide Robert Jordan with ideas and ideals which would justify his participation in the war and his submission to discipline. He had also to create a situation and characters which would account for Jordan's love for Spain and for the Spanish people. This was necessary both for the immediate purposes of plot and setting and for the thematic purpose of demonstrating the possibility of communication between men, the fraternity which is central to the novel's theme. The characters had to perform an ideological function in the novel, demonstrating the political awakening of the Spanish (and symbolically all) people, setting up ideological problems for Robert Jordan to solve, providing alternatives to his solutions of these problems, and showing the weaknesses as well as the strengths of the Loyalist side.

Beyond this, and of first importance, Hemingway had to provide the tensions and the conflicts which could test his ideas and his characters. This aspect of the political novelist's task has been described by Irving Howe: "He knows that his own momentum, his own intentions, can be set loose easily enough; but he senses, as well, that what matters most of all is to allow for those rocks against which his intentions may smash, but, if he is lucky, they may merely bruise." [22] Hemingway provides these rocks in *FWBT* in the treachery of Pablo, the frivolousness of the gypsy, Anselmo's views on killing, the behavior of men like André Marty, the humanity of the Fascist soldiers,

[22] *Politics and the Novel* (New York: Meridian Press, 1957), p. 32.

and even the necessity for submitting to Communist discipline. All of these suggest that Jordan's mission is futile or wrong, because the war may already be lost, or because nothing could justify the killing of enemies who share the common humanity. One of Hemingway's triumphs in the novel is his creation of realistic and believable "rocks," far more real and menacing than Philip Rawlings' "horrorous" or Dorothy Bridges' dubious charms. In so doing, Hemingway can draw upon the materials and themes with which he is most familiar. He succeeds also in justifying the guerillas' participation in the war, because their commitment to the Loyalist cause comes directly from their experience and because Hemingway, in a remarkable feat of characterization, endows them with a strength and indomitability which enable them to maintain their commitment despite the depredations of war. But Hemingway does not succeed in justifying Robert Jordan.

Jordan is in many ways different from other Hemingway heroes. He is given the ability to make meaningful choices, he becomes involved in the violence of war because he makes such choices rather than by accident, and he believes in what he is doing, which implies a belief that violence can have a purpose and can result in some good. Nick Adams, Jake Barnes, Frederic Henry, and Harry Morgan all find themselves thrust into violent situations. Even Pedro Romero is limited in his choices to deciding upon a setting in which to confront violence, and even this choice, as his fight with Robert Cohn shows, is not always certain. Like Jordan, Pedro Romero is committed to an ideology, but in *The Sun Also Rises* Romero's ideology is sterile, affecting only the lives of its adherents and a few others. Robert Jordan, on the other hand, confronts the possibility of death because it is his duty to mankind. In trying to describe the greatness of his love for Maria, he tells her, "I love thee as I love liberty and dignity

and the rights of all men to work and not be hungry." (p. 348)
Inappropriate as such an expression may be in a tender love
scene, it shows the way Jordan's mind works. His concern is
for the welfare of mankind, not for personal honor. The kind
of comparison he makes here would have been unthinkable
for Jake Barnes or Frederic Henry, or even for Pedro Romero.

The reasons for Jordan's devotion to duty set him apart
from the code heroes. This devotion is related to his sense
of communion with other men, and forces him to act as he is
ordered to, rather than as his emotions or his sense of honor
might direct, because he accepts the assumption that following orders will contribute to some greater good. The Hemingway code implied a special knowledge of the conditions of
life, a revelation of the imminence of violence, as well as the
special necessity for acting well in the face of danger. Hemingway's experiment in writing a code story about Spain
("The Denunciation") seems to have shown him that the
code would not serve his new purposes, and Robert Jordan
does not receive the special enlightenment normally given to
code heroes. (Such special enlightenment *is* given to the
Communists in the novel. Like those earlier characters who
lived by the code, they see reality more clearly than other
men. But Jordan, while he accepts what he is told by such
men as Golz and Karkov, is not really an "insider.") His
knowledge of the chances against success in the bridge-blowing
is shared by Pablo and Pilar and any other members of the
guerrilla band who bother to think about their task.

Jordan's distance from the code heroes is emphasized by the
fact that there are opportunities in *FWBT* for the kind of
fruitless but graceful act that would have appealed mightily
to the narrator of "The Denunciation," notably when El Sordo's band is attacked on the mountaintop. But this kind of

gesture is now referred to scornfully as the kind of thing that would appeal to Anarchists: "Whenever things get really bad they want to set fire to something and to die. It's a very odd kind of mind they have." (p. 305) Jordan does share some of the characteristics of the code heroes, notably the compulsion to exhibit physical courage, but this need cause no confusion. When he decides that he must go through with his assignment despite all the portents of failure, his sense of duty, not the need to prove himself, decides him. At the end, when he is wounded too badly to escape with the others, his insistence on remaining behind is not motivated simply by a desire to die well; his act will give the others a better chance of escaping. There is sufficient evidence to show that Jordan is a kind of hero new for Hemingway.

Having given us this different kind of hero, Hemingway is faced with the necessity of justifying him, and he tries not only to validate Jordan's actions in the immediate setting of the Spanish Civil War but to extend this validation to a larger theme, the idea that there is a solidarity among men, that "no man is an island." The chief means of presenting these ideas is through Jordan's internal monologues and dialogues, similar in tone and style to the ruminations of Jake Barnes. Hemingway's failure to present these ideas convincingly is at the heart of the novel's difficulties, and to understand the reason for this we must look closely at the action which is a frame for the ideas, action which provides the rocks which Hemingway has set in the way of his purpose. These difficulties, it should be noted, are evidence of Hemingway's realization of the requirements of the kind of political novel he was trying to write and of his confidence in his own ability as an artist to make his theme strong enough to prevail over them. The strength of the barriers he constructed is testimony also to his artistic integrity. Unlike such writers as Upton Sinclair

or William Rollins, he avoided the easy answer, the oversimplified explanation, at least in *FWBT*.

For convenience in discussion, the difficulties can be divided into two kinds, those which reveal weaknesses and failings on the Loyalist side and therefore cast doubt on the justice of the specific war Jordan is fighting in, and those which
raise the question of whether any war can be justified. In a
sense, these are the same thing. Given Hemingway's attitude
toward the Spanish Civil War, it is clear that if any war can
be justified on ideological grounds it must be this one; if this
one is simply another example of senseless violence, then all
wars must be so. In the context of the novel, however, we can
make a distinction between those problems which relate to a
particular cause and those which stand in the way of the
novel's theme, the value of human life and the traditional
democratic values.

A major difficulty of the war as Hemingway describes it is
the character of the Spanish people. Robert Jordan, like Hemingway, has a deep affection for the Spanish people, but this
does not prevent the author from including in the novel incidents which show what he regards as their natural cruelty
and callousness toward human suffering, as well as their tendency toward treachery. The treachery is spoken of directly,
in one of Jordan's internal monologues. Speculating on why
he had been accepted by the Spanish, he thinks:

He never felt like a foreigner in Spanish and they did not really
treat him like a foreigner most of the time; only when they turned
on you.

Of course they turned on you. They turned on you often but they
always turned on everyone. They turned on themselves, too. If you
had three together, two would unite against one, and then the two
would start to betray each other. Not always, but often enough for
you to take cases and start to draw it as a conclusion. (p. 135)

In the action of the novel, this judgment is borne out by Pablo's defection on the night before the bridge-blowing, and by his killing of the guerrillas from other bands whom he had recruited to help. The former action arouses Jordan: "Muck the whole treachery-ridden country. Muck their egotism and their selfishness and their egotism and their conceit and their treachery." (p. 369)

The cruelty of the Spanish people is present almost continually in *FWBT*, coming to the surface in such incidents as Pablo's killing of the other guerrillas, in Agustín's lurid plans for punishing the Fascists after the war (p. 369), in certain aspects of Pilar's treatment of Maria, and, most sharply, in Pilar's description of the killing of the Fascists in her town at the beginning of the movement. (pp. 99–129) The method of execution she describes is so brutal that it disgusts everyone but the drunks, the Anarchists, and Pablo, but the violence generates its own momentum. There is universality in this scene of mob violence, emphasized by Robert Jordan's recollection of a lynching, but its special Spanish character is clear in Pablo's behavior after the killing is done: he is spent as a bullfighter is spent after a corrida, and ashamed that the priest tried to run at the end: "He was a *Spanish* priest." (p. 128) This scene, as described by Pilar, is one of the most memorable in the novel, and it helps to point out that atrocities are in the nature of war, not the exclusive property of one side or the other. At the end of Pilar's narrative, Hemingway tries to moderate what amounts to a criticism of the Loyalists by having Pilar say that the only worse day of her life was "Three days later when the fascists took the town." (p. 129) For once, however, Hemingway's favorite device of understatement is ineffective. The scenes described by Pilar remain in the reader's mind.

Hemingway also raises the problem of the political dis-

putes among the Loyalists. At least in part, this is done to take
the curse off Robert Jordan's acceptance of Communist discipline, and most of the criticism is directed against the Communists. Other groups come in for critical comment, too, especially the Anarchists, and in the course of one of the abortive
political discussions which checker the novel, Agustín puts a
curse on all their houses, "And afterwards shoot the anarchists
and the Communists and all this *canalla* except the good Republicans" (p. 285), but the Communists receive the lion's
share. The most striking instances of this are the savage attacks on the idols of the Comintern, André Marty and La
Pasionaria (Dolores Ibarruri). The French hero is dragged
into the narrative when he provides one of the hindrances to
Andrés' attempt, late in the novel, to get a message through
to General Golz. Marty is clearly insane, convinced that
"the rot" of treason touches everyone but himself, and he is
charged with responsibility for the execution of many of the
men in the International Brigades on charges of political devi-
ation. It may be this last activity that roused Hemingway's
ire, since he had earlier shown, in the short story "Under the
Ridge," his low opinion of the battlefield police. His description of Marty is evidently accurate; a number of other writers
have given similar portrayals of the hero of Kronstadt and his
behavior in Spain. In any case, Hemingway's attack on Marty
is savage and bitter, and it is germane to the action only as
it tends to show that not all Loyalists were among nature's
noblemen.

La Pasionaria does not directly interfere with the prosecution of the war, in *FWBT*, but Hemingway obviously regards
her as a handicap to the Loyalist cause. He puts his criticism
of her in the ironic words of Karkov, Jordan's political men-
tor, who remains unmoved by an *Izvestia* correspondent's description of "that great voice where pity, compassion and truth

are blended." (p. 357) " 'That great voice,' Karkov said. 'That great face. Write it,' he said. 'Don't tell it to me. Don't waste whole paragraphs on me. Go and write it now.' " (p. 358) Pasionaria is a publicity heroine, of no use where the war is being fought. The last point is made clear late in the novel, in the narrative of El Sordo's last stand. The boy Joaquin has substituted the propaganda image of Pasionaria for the religious image of the Virgin, but doubt is cast on his new idol by other members of the band who do not share the Communist faith: " 'Do you know your Pasionaria has a son thy age in Russia since the start of the movement?' " " 'If thou believest so much in thy Pasionaria, get her to get us off this hill . . .' " (p. 309) Joaquin's repetition of one of the party's slogans, *"Resistir y fortificar es vencer,"* and of Pasionaria's own slogan, "It is better to die on your feet than to live on your knees," is greeted by his colleagues with a single word: " *'Mierda.'* " (p. 309) At the end his new idol is insufficient to sustain the boy; when the bombs begin to fall he changes his prayer from " 'Pasionaria says "Better to die on thy —" ' " to " 'Hail Mary, full of grace . . .' " (p. 321) In extremities, the new saint is less comforting than the old.

Hemingway's savagery in attacking Marty and Pasionaria seems to be both an expression of personal animosity and another gambit in that favorite indoor sport of the Spanish Civil War, dissociating oneself from undesirable elements. In the context of the novel, these attacks have a more immediate purpose as revelations of the weaknesses of even that party which provides the best discipline and the best program for winning the war. The failings of the Communists are brought out also in the two pictures of their informal headquarters, Gaylord's in Madrid. On the night before the offensive, it is clear that in this exclusive club there is too much loose talk, too much naïveté, too little consciousness that the war is a

serious business, not a sport. Karkov's mistress asks if she
can go with him to the offensive, as if it were a kind of game
to watch. (pp. 356–59) In Robert Jordan's reminiscences of
his own visits to Gaylord's, this frivolousness is not so obtrusive, but he himself views the fact of his going to Gaylord's
as part of the process of disillusionment. Baker points out
that a tension exists in the novel between the idealism represented by the International Brigade headquarters and the
cynical realism represented by Gaylord's (pp. 241–45), but
he mistakenly maintains that Jordan retains his balance between these two poles. Jordan accepts the lessons of Gaylord's,
including the knowledge that the popular heroes are bad generals, the realization that many of the "peasant" and "worker"
officers speak fluent Russian, and the interpretations of political matters fed to him by Karkov. All this is presented as
part of learning what war is all about:

Gaylord's was good and sound and what he needed. At the start when
he had still believed all the nonsense it had come as a shock to him.
But now he knew enough to accept the necessity for all the deception
and what he learned at Gaylord's only strengthened him in his belief
in the things that he did hold to be true. (p. 230)

In his musings at the front, Jordan associates Gaylord's with
corruption. It serves the useful function of providing a realistic picture of the circumstances of the war in Spain, but it also
reveals unpleasant truths about the Communist proconsuls and
their sycophants. In the novel, Gaylord's is another artistic
obstacle.

Finally, there is the fact that Jordan is fighting in a losing
cause. The military effort of the Loyalists is inadequate: partly
the result of the sectarian corruption symbolized by Gaylord's,
partly the fault of the Spanish people. But the Loyalists are
woefully short of material, and even when they are well armed

they seldom use their weapons wisely. Jordan is continually concerned with the problem of discipline, because the Loyalists have so little of it: "He was very happy with that sudden, rare happiness that can come to any one with a command in a revolutionary army; the happiness of finding that even one of your flanks holds." (p. 199) The military inadequacies of the Loyalists reach from the lowest ranks to the highest, from Fernando's abandonment of his post to catch some rabbits, to Golz's inability to get the necessary artillery support for his offensive, to the insanity of André Marty which assures that the futile attack will be carried out.

These difficulties, serious as they are, are still peculiar to the war in Spain. In order to universalize his material, Hemingway also considers the larger problem of whether any war can be justified, whether any killing is right or even excusable. It is a problem he had never really investigated before his experience in the Spanish Civil War. Always before, in Hemingway's fiction, violent death had been almost a natural phenomenon, a condition of modern life. Now his hero must deal death, deliberately, in a new kind of situation. The morality of killing, even in a just cause, is mentioned so often in *FWBT* as to be almost an obsession.

The old man, Anselmo, states the question bluntly. He has been a hunter, and unlike Robert Jordan has gotten pleasure from killing animals, but he is deeply disturbed by the necessity for killing men. He has killed, he says: "Several times, but not with pleasure. To me it is a sin to kill a man. Even Fascists whom we must kill. To me there is a great difference between the bear and the man and I do not believe the wizardry of the gypsies about the brotherhood with animals. No. I am against all killing of men." (p. 41) Anselmo has abandoned his religion, but he still regards killing as a mortal sin, and he feels the need to do "something very strong to atone for it." (p. 197) In the bridge-blowing, Anselmo is forced to kill, but he does so only under a direct order, and he is not really reconciled:

I hated the shooting of the guard and it made me an emotion but that is passed now. How could the Inglés say that the shooting of a man is like the shooting of an animal? In all hunting I have had an elation and no feeling of wrong. But to shoot a man gives a feeling as though one had struck one's own brother when you are grown men. And to shoot him various times to kill him. (p. 442)

Anselmo is at one pole. At the other is Agustín, who also feels an emotion associated with killing: "And when I saw those four there and thought that we might kill them I was like a mare in the corral waiting for the stallion . . . the necessity was on me as it is on a mare in heat. You cannot know what it is if you have not felt it." (p. 286) Jordan at first tries to explain this away as a peculiarly Spanish reaction ("It is their extra sacrament"), but he too has felt it:

Stop making dubious literature about the Berbers and the old Iberians and admit that you have liked to kill as all who are soldiers by choice have enjoyed it at some time whether they lie about it or not. . . . Don't lie to yourself, he thought. Nor make up literature about it. You have been tainted with it for a long time now. (p. 287)

Jordan is neither Anselmo nor Agustín. He does not feel the sickness which Anselmo experiences when the necessity for killing confronts him; not only is he able to kill, he is able to order others to do so. On the other hand, he does share Anselmo's distaste for bloodshed, and while he knows the blood lust of Agustín, he also knows that it is dangerous. After he has shot the young enemy cavalryman from Tafalla who rides into the guerrillas' clearing, he warns himself that when killing becomes enjoyable, or an end in itself, it is disastrous:

It is right, he told himself, not reassuringly but proudly. I believe in the people and their right to govern themselves as they wish. But you mustn't believe in killing, he told himself. You must do it as a necessity but you must not believe in it. If you believe in it the whole thing is wrong. (p. 304)

This is a far cry from the Philip Rawlings of *The Fifth Column*, who decidedly enjoyed killing. Hemingway, for whom hunting had always been the most enjoyable of sports, and upon whom war and death had always exerted an unusual fascination, had in Spain been confronted with the moral problems of war in a way not suggested in his earlier work. Hemingway tries very hard in *FWBT* to show that killing cannot be justified in Agustín's terms, and that Anselmo's objections are of fundamental importance: "You have no right to do the things you do for all of them are crimes and no man has a right to take another man's life unless it is to prevent something worse happening to other people." (p. 304)

The care with which Hemingway has considered the question of killing in this novel is further indicated by the fact that the "Fascists" in the novel are deliberately made men like any others. Whenever the reader is given more than a passing glimpse of the men on the Insurgent side, these men are Spaniards, sharing the ethnic traits of the Loyalists. One critic has maintained that this is a distortion of the facts of the war: "The tremendous support of Franco by the Axis through diplomatic pressure and armed intervention plays no part in the narrative."[23] This is only partly true, since it ignores the frightening presence of the German Heinkel bombers in the novel. Even if it were true, however, the charge does not apply to a novel as it would to a history of the war; Hemingway in this instance chose to give far more attention to the human

[23] Edwin Berry Burgum, "Ernest Hemingway and the Psychology of the Lost Generation," in McCaffery, p. 327.

dilemmas involved in a civil war, and less to political facts. In so doing he chose the truth of art rather than the truth of historical fact.

Jordan's reading of the letter found in the wallet of the Navarrese soldier is only one instance of Hemingway's pattern of showing the similarity between the men fighting on different sides. An earlier example is the abrupt shift of point of view from Anselmo, watching a Fascist outpost, to the men in the outpost itself, whose conversation closely parallels that of the guerrillas, even to their shared fear of airplanes. (pp. 195–96) The point is driven home by Hemingway's use of the Insurgent Lieutenant Berrendo. After the battle in which his men and the airplanes have destroyed El Sordo's band, he grieves for the death of his friend, gives Joaquin the *coup de grâce* "as quickly and as gently" as he can, and after reluctantly issuing orders for the decapitation of the dead, muses on "What a bad thing war is," leaving before the men carry out his orders. (p. 322) His thoughts after battle are similar to Jordan's. (p. 326) And it is Berrendo whom the doomed Jordan is preparing to kill in the novel's final scene.

If *FWBT* were a study in moral complexity, an investigation of the ironies and contradictions inherent in wars and in ideologies, the problem of justifying violence might well be one of the book's strong points. But Hemingway's purpose is to show the reader that Jordan's actions are morally right, because he is partaking in a just and necessary fight, and so, in Howe's metaphor, the moral dilemma of violence becomes one of the rocks past which the author must steer his craft. If the people of Spain are cruel and treacherous, if their leaders are corrupt and stupid, if the only group which offers a sensible program for winning the war is a haven for fools, madmen, and cynics, and if killing is always wrong, then the motives for Jordan's actions must be convincing indeed. That they are not is the measure of the novel's failure.

This is not to say that Hemingway is totally unsuccessful. He is able to justify Jordan's affection for the Spanish people, not only in Jordan's meditations on their virtues and their faults, but in the action of the novel as well. They are cruel and treacherous, but they are also courageous, generous, and frequently loyal. The battle on the hilltop shows the ineffectuality of Joaquin's faith in Pasionaria, but it also demonstrates the shrewdness, humor, and valor of El Sordo himself. Pablo's band is weakened by the presence of Pablo and the gypsy, but it has also the strength of Pilar, Anselmo, the stupid but courageous Fernando, and the quiet brothers, Andrés and Eladio. Jordan's affection for these people is real and understandable. The difficulty is that, given the conditions he has presented, Hemingway cannot expect simple human affection to carry the whole weight of his theme.

When he tries to impart the rest of the message, the idea that a particular side in a particular war is right, Hemingway relies almost entirely on the thoughts he places in the mind of Robert Jordan. This in itself is a weakness, since it means, as Geismar pointed out long ago, that the ideological point of the novel does not arise out of the action; it is rather imposed upon the action through Jordan's conversation and his thoughts.[24] Still, the message might have been effective had Hemingway been able to make the expression of his ideas strong enough. But Robert Jordan seems not really sure of his reasons for fighting. He questions his own motives when he makes himself admit that he shares Agustín's blood lust at the prospect of killing, and throughout the book he cautions himself not to romanticize himself or the Spanish people. He does so in such a way as to convince the reader that, whatever

[24] Geismar, *Writers in Crisis*, pp. 81–83.

his reasons, they are probably as shallowly sentimental as he himself fears they are.

Jordan's uncertainty is revealed whenever another character brings up the question of war aims. When he first considers the problem he simply dismisses it: "And what about a planned society and the rest of it? That was for the others to do. He had something else to do after the war." (p. 163) Later on, he acquires a rather narrow purpose: what he wants out of the war is the chance to take Maria back to Madrid with him and to hobnob again with the boys at Gaylord's. As the book draws to a close he returns to the problem again, and significantly his thoughts have nothing to do with Spain; he has evaded the problem of the aims of the present conflict by going on to a larger area:

> But remember this that as long as we can hold them here we keep the fascists tied up. They can't attack any other country until they finish with us. If the French help at all, if only they leave the frontier open and if we get planes from America they can never finish with us. Never, if we get anything at all. These people will fight forever if they're well armed.
>
> No you must not expect victory here, not for several years maybe. This is just a holding attack. You must not get illusions about it now. (p. 432)

Jordan returns to this conception of the war when he lies in the forest waiting for death: "If we win here we will win everywhere. The world is a fine place and worth fighting for and I hate very much to leave it." (p. 467)

Through statements like this, Jordan is shown to be extremely vague and changeable about his war aims. At one time he has none, at another his desires are extremely limited, at yet another they are all-embracing. At no time do they relate specifically to the war in Spain or to the Spanish people. The poverty of Jordan's notions of what the war might bring is emphasized by Anselmo's statement of his hopes: "That we should win this war and shoot nobody. . . . That we should govern justly and that all should participate in the benefits according as they have striven for them. And that those who have fought against us should be educated to see their error." (p. 285)

Such a simple statement, however, cannot serve for a character who is supposed to be as highly sophisticated as is Jordan, and Hemingway is reduced to presenting Jordan's case in abstract terms. Since his hero is not committed to any particular political dogma, the author cannot present a doctrinaire program, and what is left is unsatisfactory. Too sophisticated, too familiar with violence to have retained the quasi-religious feeling about the war he had known earlier (pp. 235–48), Jordan is reduced to clichés: "You believe in Liberty, Equality and Fraternity. You believe in Life, Liberty, and the Pursuit of Happiness." (p. 305)

When Hemingway relies upon such terms in explaining his hero, he is doing precisely what he had objected to so vehemently in his famous denunciation of abstractions in *A Farewell To Arms*. One critic has noted how inadequate this type of expression is in the circumstances:

. . . It is a failure, not because it is an affirmative value, not because it is a patriotic sentiment, but because it is conventional and trite. When he says "You believe in Liberty, Equality and Fraternity. You believe in Life, Liberty and the Pursuit of Happiness," the author is attempting to rely only upon generalities which, admirable as they may be as a statement or even as symbols of democracy, are not sharp enough to carry the emotional weight put upon them.[25]

To put it in terms of this study, when it comes to giving his hero an ideological justification Hemingway is no more so-

[25] Ray B. West, "Ernest Hemingway: The Failure of Sensibility," in William Van O'Connor, ed., *Forms of Modern Fiction* (Minneapolis: University of Minnesota Press, 1948), p. 95.

phisticated or convincing than Upton Sinclair. When Jordan talks this way he seems to have reverted to his time of inno- cence (associated in the novel with the International Brigade headquarters) before he knew the realities of the war. By the time Jordan uses this explanation, both he and the reader are fully aware of the realities, and the phrases used will not serve.

This example is only one of a number of attempts Heming- way makes in the novel to formulate an ideology for Jordan. Whenever Jordan's ideas about the war are made to seem important, Hemingway falls back on internal monologues which were terse and appropriate to Jake Barnes, but which in *FWBT* are rambling and sophomoric. Even less successful are the "You-he" dialogues between Jordan and his better self. It does not seem to me to be enough to argue, as has Joseph Warren Beach, that there is irony in Hemingway's view of Jordan's formulations, that both author and hero are aware that the formulations are thin, and that they are intended primarily to suggest the depth of Jordan's (and Hemingway's) feeling for the Republic. Beach is persuasive, not least when he argues that "what [Hemingway] thinks he has found, in the Spanish War, is social or moral ideals to which one can devote oneself wholeheartedly and without giving up a real- istic understanding of the ways of the world."[26]

Unfortunately, the effect of Jordan's self-justification is not to give the impression of one who has actually *found* ideals worthy of wholehearted devotion. It is rather to indicate that neither author nor hero is sure of his ground, that while he wishes for certitude he is constantly aware of doubts in his own mind. The condition Mr. Beach describes applies to the Hemingway who wrote *The Fifth Column*, the dispatches to

[26] Joseph Warren Beach, "How Do You Like It Now, Gentlemen," in *Hemingway and His Critics*, Carlos Baker, ed. (New York: Hill & Wang, 1961), p. 240.

Ken, and "The Denunciation," not to the man who wrote *FWBT*. By the time he wrote the novel, Hemingway had seen enough of violence committed in the name of ideology to have become conscious again of the truth of Orwell's dictum that "bullets hurt and corpses stink" whether the cause one is fighting for is good or evil. The easy, almost complacent self-justifications of Rawlings, or of such figures as the hero of Sinclair's novel, at this later stage must have seemed hollow to Hemingway. At the same time he was still to some extent affected by the excitement of the war and by the sensation of being "on the inside," conferred on him by his friend Mikhail Kolzov, so that he felt it necessary to try to provide Jordan with an ideological justification. Even if we accept Beach's argument that Hemingway was aware of the weakness of Jordan's case, we can still argue that Hemingway's own ambivalence about the Spanish Civil War has resulted in an uneasy and debilitating compromise in the novel.

The novel's ideological difficulties are compounded by the problems attendant upon Hemingway's theme, the oneness of mankind. Ultimately, the ideological concept that this war is worth fighting and winning rests upon the thematic conception that all men are one, that "any man's death diminishes me." Hemingway, whose integrity as an artist is beyond challenge, does what he must do in extending this concept to include the enemy. Since he has made it clear that the Loyalist side has no more a monopoly on virtue than the Fascists have on evil, and since he takes considerable care to show that in many ways the Fascists are indistinguishable from the Loyalists as people, Hemingway makes it very difficult for the reader to accept the notion that the way to human brotherhood is through killing Fascists, who as it turns out are usually not Fascists anyway. The reader is left with the uneasy conviction that if Hemingway's theme is valid his ideological justification for Jordan's action cannot be.

The problems of theme in the novel go deeper than this. Hemingway tries valiantly to make his story a demonstration of the concept of oneness. This is, I believe, the reason for the broad canvas of the novel, with its abandonment of Hemingway's favored first-person narrator so that the third-person narrator can move away from Robert Jordan and the guerilla camp to Sordo's last stand, to the Fascist outpost, to the minds of the Fascist soldiers, to Golz's command post, to Madrid. In certain incidents the theme receives special emphasis, most strikingly in the generally ignored description of the handshake in the dark between Robert Jordan and Pablo before the attack on the bridge:

> Robert Jordan, when he put his hand out, expected that it would be like grasping something reptilian or touching a leper. He did not know what Pablo's hand would feel like. But in the dark Pablo's hand gripped his hard and pressed it frankly and he returned the grip. Pablo had a good hand in the dark and it gave Robert Jordan the strangest feeling he had felt that morning. We must be allies now, he thought. (p. 404)

In the development of the novel, however, the weight of the theme rests less on such explicit interludes than on the relationship between Robert Jordan and Maria. Their affair is given so much attention in the novel that one Communist critic has been moved to object that ". . . the shattering struggle of twenty-eight million people for survival and decency was subordinated to an endless episode in a sleeping bag, and the phrase 'the earth moved' was quoted by bohemians and bourgeois with a leer on their faces."[27] Such a complaint is valid

[27] Alvah Bessie, *The Un-Americans* (London: John Calder, 1957), pp. 211–12.

only if the novel's theme is ignored; a more just objection is
that the affair does not achieve its purpose, that the relationship
between Jordan and Maria is so determinedly sexual that the
reader is never convinced by it that men (and/or women) can
communicate on any but the most primitive levels.

It is absolutely necessary to the meaning of the novel that
the relationship between Jordan and Maria should show that
they are truly one, as they tell each other they are (p. 262)
and as Jordan reminds Maria when she must leave him to
his solitary death (p. 463.) But they are never one except on
a sexual level, a fact which is made brutally clear soon after
the earth has moved. When the two are returning from the
historic field to the guerrillas' cave, Jordan's mind goes to work
and when she tries to share his thoughts, he tells Maria that
"What I do now I do alone and very coldly in my head." (p.
172) Jordan's rejection of the girl as anything but a sexual
object could not be more clear.

Jordan can hardly be blamed for his attitude, for despite
the attempts of critics to inflate Maria into a symbol of almost
everything,[28] she is such a pallid figure, particularly when
seen next to Pilar, that she hardly seems human at all. Jordan
calls her his "rabbit," a term which would have been highly
insulting to any Spanish woman.[29] Even in its literal American
meaning, the word alludes to an animal that is furry, unintel-
ligent, and reputed to have a remarkable proclivity for copula-
tion and reproduction. Maria may be sterile as the result of

[28] See, for example, Frederic I. Carpenter, "Hemingway Achieves the
Fifth Dimension," in *Hemingway and His Critics*, Carlos Baker, ed., espe-
cially p. 198; see also Joseph Warren Beach, "How Do You Like It Now,
Gentlemen," in the same volume, pp. 227–44.

[29] Arturo Barea, "Not Spain But Hemingway," *Horizon*, III (May,
1941), 359–60. This essay also appears in Baker's collection. Barea notes
that this is an especially unfortunate error resulting from Hemingway's
ignorance of colloquial Spanish, in which the word for "rabbit" is also
the word for the female genitalia.

her earlier experiences, but in other respects the nickname is all too apt.

The problems created by this love affair are not alleviated by the fact that Hemingway is trying to use the sexual relationship in a way entirely different from anything he had attempted before. In *FWBT*, sex is intended to symbolize a broad human relationship, where always before it had been used to represent a kind of anodyne which provides only temporary solace and no more than an illusion of communication. Implicit in *The Sun Also Rises, A Farewell to Arms*, and a number of Hemingway's short stories is the idea that sex does *not* serve as a substitute for other kinds of communication, and in fact those characters in the earlier works who put too much of themselves into a purely sexual relationship are generally trapped by it, like Frederic Henry and Catherine Barkley, or the young couple of "Hills Like White Elephants."

If Hemingway's new conception of sex as a metaphor of communication is to be successful, an entirely new kind of heroine (for Hemingway) is needed, one who can communicate with her lover on other levels than the sexual, but this is a creature that he was apparently unable to create. Instead we have one more erotic daydream, entirely too much like Catherine Barkley. While it has been argued that Catherine influences her lover to withdraw from the war and Maria "strengthens and inspires her lover for his social service,"[30] this is not adequate to the demands placed upon her. There is also, of course, a kind of horrible irony in the description of Jordan's job as a "social service," when it consists of blowing up bridges and killing men whom the author has been at pains to show are the hero's brothers.

The difficulties of Maria's role are not materially improved by Jordan's speculations on the possibility of living a lifetime

[30] Theodore Bardacke, "Hemingway's Women," in McCaffery, p. 350.

in a few days or hours. When Jordan says to himself "you had better love her very hard and make up in intensity what the relation will lack in duration and in continuity" (p. 168), or when he speculates that it may be "possible to live as full a life in seventy hours as in seventy years" (p. 166), we are made aware of Hemingway's uncertainties about the role of the love affair and his attempts to strengthen it. But these attempts do nothing to strengthen Maria as a character. She was certainly the kind of woman Robert Jordan needed on his last mission, but she is emphatically not the kind of woman the theme of this novel demands.

And the theme is unsatisfactory. Nowhere is this more clear than in the novel's conclusion, for Robert Jordan is left to face death alone, like any other Hemingway hero. The love affair does not convince us that Maria's continued existence means that Jordan will also go on living; rather, it is clear that his desperate pleading with her is based upon an unselfish desire to get her out of danger and a selfish wish to be left to die alone, not on his belief that what he tells her is true. When Maria and the others have left, Jordan goes through a series of mental gymnastics while awaiting the Fascist soldiers, an attempt at reconciling himself to his fate which casts grave doubts on the accuracy of the author's flat statement, "he was completely integrated now. . . ." (p. 471) When everything is finished, the theme of the novel is more like the old Hemingway lesson that it is futile to kick against the pricks than the explicit lesson of *FWBT* that all men are brothers. Robert Jordan dies, and his success in blowing the bridge is hollow because the offensive itself is a disaster. The war, as Hemingway knew when he wrote the book, was lost. As a result, the only consolations that can legitimately be given to Robert Jordan are the purely personal ones: he knows that he acted well and he had found a woman to love.

FWBT deserves extended analysis because it demonstrates so clearly the dilemma of writers who continued to believe in the Loyalist cause, but who had seen and understood too much to be capable of the easy sophistries of the authors discussed earlier. They tried to avoid the simple black and white distinctions, and to look behind the political slogans to the realities they had themselves witnessed, an attempt in which they were not always successful. Their disillusion had not yet turned to bitterness, and when they despaired they often tried to cloak that despair with other themes; as *FWBT* shows, the result was often a failure. The symbols and the slogans which had seemed so pure to more innocent writers had become blurred in battle, and when they reverted to such symbols they often had a nostalgic quality.

5. Bullets Hurt, Corpses Stink

DURING the Spanish Civil War, and in some cases even after the defeat of the Loyalists, writers like those discussed in the previous chapter were able to find grounds for faith in the Loyalist cause even though they were sickened by war and, in some cases, by what they knew of Loyalist politics. If their side was losing, it might yet be saved by any of a number of events; if the cause was lost, it might be revived again when the Spanish people had had enough of tyranny or when other nations at last realized what had been at stake in Spain. In either case, for all its faults the Republic was a just cause, and worth the sacrifices it demanded. Not surprisingly, other writers were far less sanguine, and attached more importance to the death of their hopes, the hard realities of war, and the disillusioning political mess than to slogans and beliefs which came to seem empty or irrelevant to their experiences.

For most such writers, the violence and dislocation of the war were crucial. The actual experience of battle, for all that young intellectuals might have learned of it vicariously from the realistic literature of World War I, was indubitably a

shock. This is conveyed most clearly, perhaps, by a poem supposedly found on a leaf of notebook paper by a soldier in
the International Brigades, and subsequently printed in the
Spender-Lehmann anthology, *Poems for Spain*:

> Eyes of men running, falling, screaming
> Eyes of men shouting, sweating, bleeding
> The eyes of the fearful, those of the sad
> The eyes of exhaustion, and those of the mad
> Eyes of men thinking, hoping, waiting
> Eyes of men loving, cursing, hating
> The eyes of the wounded sodden in red
> The eyes of the dying and those of the dead.[1]

The same spirit of revulsion is found in the same volume in
the writings of such soldier poets as John Lepper and T. A. R.
Hyndman. It finds its most vehement expression, however, in
the poems of Stephen Spender.

Spender was obviously deeply affected by the Spanish War,
despite the fact that he took no part in the actual fighting. His
reaction to the political and social climate of the thirties had
always been more extreme than the reactions of his friends
and colleagues, Auden, Day Lewis, MacNeice, and Rex
Warner, and the pattern did not change when the Spanish
Civil War broke out. Among other things, Spender permitted
himself to be enrolled in the Communist party, and his induc-
tion was carried out by no less a figure than Harry Pollitt.
The rather special circumstances and special terms of this
arrangement were objectionable to other party members, and
the whole process was faintly similar to some of Fulton Sheen's
conversions to Catholicism among American intellectuals.[2]

[1] Stephen Spender and John Lehmann, eds., *Poems for Spain* (London:
Hogarth Press, 1939), p. 31. For information about the poem's discovery,
see John Lehmann, *The Whispering Gallery* (New York: Harcourt, Brace,
1955), p. 281.

[2] Stephen Spender, *World Within World*, p. 192.

Despite the suspicions of hardened party members that he was no more than a dilettante, Spender took his new obligations seriously. He wrote articles and reviews for *Left Review*, he made several trips to Spain, and he put considerable effort into the job of editing *Poems for Spain*. In his introduction to that volume, he even made a pass at writing a "Poetics" for an "orthodox communist poetry."

Spender's autobiographical descriptions of these quasi-revolutionary activities reveal clearly the dilemmas of the modern intellectual, especially during the thirties. His belief in his own intelligence and personal inviolability is balanced precariously against the attractions of a firm commitment to a dogmatic belief (in Spender's case, communism), which, if he can make himself accept it, will ease many of his problems. Personal relationships frequently exert a force opposite to that of his belief. War is good and/or bad in the abstract, depending upon particular circumstance, but war in reality is a dreadful thing, and therefore evil. Literature is important in itself, but the survival of civilization, of mankind itself, is obviously more important, and literature like any other activity should be used to advance the cause. Spender was subject to all these forces and to the doubts they raised, but in the middle and late thirties he undertook activities which reflect a sincere desire to implement his commitment to the class war and to the future it promised to bring.

At the same time, it is clear in his prose as well as his poems that Spender never felt at ease in the world of politics. His own poems, including those dealing with the war in Spain, indicate that while he might hope for an "orthodox communist poetry," he never aspired to be its originator. His prose reflects doubts about some of his comrades and colleagues. In writing of the famous Writers' Congress, held in Madrid and Valencia in 1937, he manages to reveal the silly self-importance of

André Chamson and the frivolity of the concerns of most of the conferees, as well as the nasty political chicanery carried on in the name of idealism.[3] He also indicates his considerable horror at the hardness of a literary figure (evidently Ralph Bates) who, as an officer in the Republican Army, showed less interest in and compassion for the men in his command than he had for the characters in his novels.

These facts help to explain why Spender's poems on the Spanish War exemplify an extreme reaction, especially if it is kept in mind that Spender never was an intellectual poet. He might have entertained intellectual doubts about his commitment to communism, but on the whole he could believe that such a commitment was necessary. Emotionally, he could only be shocked and horrified by what he saw in Spain. Even while he wrote his introduction to *Poems for Spain*, his own poems were expressing revulsion against the violence and cruelty of war. None of his four poems chosen for inclusion in that volume expresses anything like a "correct" ideology, and their common themes are death and destruction.

Of the ten poems about Spain which Spender later chose to include in *Collected Poems*, only one makes any overt statement of sympathy for the Loyalists. "Fall of a City" gives a picture of desolation and loss following an Insurgent victory. The words and deeds of the Loyalists, the deaths of men like Ralph Fox and Federico García Lorca, are "washed over with a smile / Which launches the victors where they win."[4] The only consolation is that in defeat some memory of liberty may remain to inspire future generations:

> . . . Somewhere some word presses
> In the high door of a skull, and in some corner
> Of an irrefrangible eye

[3] *Ibid.*, pp. 220–24.
[4] Stephen Spender, *Collected Poems*, pp. 104–05.

> Some old man's memory jumps to a child
> — Spark from the days of liberty.
> And the child hoards it like a bitter toy.

This is hardly wild-eyed propaganda, but it is as far in that direction as Spender ever went in his poetry, however militant he may sometimes have been in his prose. In his other poems about Spain he is entirely concerned with the personal rather than the public aspects of the war.

Most of the other poems express a concern about the waste of war, the waste of effort, and of life itself. "The Room Above" is a lament for a lover who has departed for "sunbright peninsulas of the sword."[5] "Thoughts During an Air Raid" considers the impersonality of statistics and casualty lists, and the fact that only a sense of personal loss can make clear the meaning of such statistics:

> . . . The essential is
> That every "one" should remain separate
> Propped up under roses, and no one suffer
> For his neighbor. Then horror is postponed
> Piecemeal for each, until it settles on him
> That wreath of incommunicable grief
> Which is all mystery or nothing.[6]

The irony of these poems stems from the bitterness which was Spender's most important legacy from his experiences in Spain, and which pervades all of these poems. Death for a cause might be attractive in the abstract, but as reality it was appalling. "A Stopwatch and an Ordinance Map," "In No Man's Land," and "Ultima Ratio Regum," all voice the question made explicit in the latter:

> Consider his life which was valueless
> In terms of employment, hotel ledgers, news files.

[5] *Collected Poems*, p. 81.
[6] *Collected Poems*, p. 96.

> Consider. One bullet in ten thousand kills a man.
> Ask. Was so much expenditure justified
> On the death of one so young and so silly
> Lying under the olive trees, O world, O death? [7]

Spender seems to have been very nearly overwhelmed by the fact of death. Ideology fades out of these poems as violent death becomes an evil more immediate and therefore more terrible than political oppression or economic exploitation. In "Two Armies," [8] Spender's subject is the eventual hatred of war itself felt by every soldier: "each man hated the cause and distant words / That brought him here . . ." Only a harsh discipline "which holds them at the point of a revolver" keeps the men from deserting. The final stanzas of "Two Armies" paint an utterly bleak picture of soldiers drained by war of every emotion, no longer able even to feel hate for the enemy:

> Finally they cease to hate; for although hate
> Bursts from the air and whips the earth with hail
> Or shoots it up in fountains to marvel at,
> And although hundreds fall, who can connect
> The inexhaustible anger of the guns
> With the dumb patience of those tormented animals?
>
> Clean silence drops at night, when a little walk
> Divides the sleeping armies, each
> Huddled in linens woven by remote hands.
> When the machines are still, a common suffering
> Whitens the air with breath and makes both one
> As though these enemies slept in each other's arms.
>
> Only the lucid friend to aerial raiders
> The brilliant pilot moon, stares down

[7] *Collected Poems*, p. 99. Published in *Poems for Spain* as "Regum Ultimo Ratio."

[8] *Collected Poems*, pp. 97–98.

> Upon this plain she makes a shining bone
> Cut by the shadows of many thousand bones.
> Where amber clouds scatter on No-Man's-Land
> She regards death and time throw up
> The furious words and minerals which destroy.

In such a poem men are no longer really responsible for anything, even for the destruction of their nominal enemies. The menace of modern war, of death-dealing machines run mad and out of control, is made clearer here than in Spender's other poems, but all these poems voice the same agonized cry: reason and decency have departed the world, and man is faced with absolute chaos. In a lyric like "Ultima Ratio Regum," the poet apostrophizes the world and death, rather than men, because men are so infected by the insanity of war that they can hear nothing but their own howls of rage and anguish. They cannot be reached, even by the poet's voice; they can only die. In the world of these poems, hatred and violence are no longer the products of human emotions: they have an independent existence, and they have also a continually accelerating momentum.

The nature of chaos is made explicit in the poem "To a Spanish Poet (Manuel Altolaguirre)." Here the poet's fear for the life of his friend leads him to an analysis of the state of the world which makes such fears inevitable:

> Perhaps it is we — the living — who are dead
> We of a world that revolves and dissolves
> While we set the steadfast corpse under the earth's lid.
> The eyes push irises above the grave
> Reaching to the stars, which draw down nearer,
> Staring through a rectangle of night like black glass,
> Beyond these daylight comedies of falling plaster.
>
> Your heart looks through the breaking ribs —
> Oiled axle through revolving spokes.

Unbroken blood of the swift wheel,
You stare through centrifugal bones
Of the revolving and dissolving world.[9]

This poem is the clearest manifestation of the effect that the horror of the war in Spain had upon Spender. He is still in control of his verse, on a technical level. The imagery, however, is unusually chaotic for Spender, as though only the images of madness could convey what he had felt and seen in Spain.

"Two Armies" and "To a Spanish Poet" are on a different level from Spender's other poetry of the Spanish War. These poems all share a preoccupation with death, but these two are evidence that in some extremity of horror or disgust the poet moved beyond pity and self-pity to a deeper perception of reality. A kind of sentimentalism pervades a good many of Spender's poems, as if he were enjoying his emotional involvement even as he felt genuine sorrow. In these two poems, however, Spender reached a more profound level to convey a naked emotional experience. They are among the most important works of the Spanish War.

Spender saw no service as a soldier, and some might regard the horror he felt as the rather timid response of a civilian who was more at home in the drawing room than on a battlefield. As I have already noted, however, the same horror at events in Spain shared by such fighting men as Hyndman, Lepper, and the anonymous author of "Eyes." It was also felt by an American, Alvah Bessie, who arrived in time to take part in the disastrous campaigns around the Ebro River in 1938, and who lived to write about his experiences in *Men in Battle*. Like John Sommerfield, Bessie was a dedicated Communist, who went to Spain to serve his party and advance the revolution, but the books of the two men are so different that they seem to record events that took place in different worlds.

[9] *Collected Poems*, p. 109.

The two memoirs create a convenient measure of the distance between the world of the men who fought in Spain at the beginning of the war and those who were there at the end. Where Sommerfield records the exciting victories of 1936, Bessie ends his book with the evacuation of foreign volunteers, that last desperate move by the Loyalist government to win sympathy and help from France, Great Britain, and the United States. The men who were shipped out then knew a great deal more about war and defeat than Sommerfield could possibly have known.

Bessie's book is not distinguished in style or in structure. His prose is generally clear, with few blatant imitations of Hemingway and none of the flights of rhapsodic impressionism in which such writers as Sommerfield and Elliott Paul took delight, but there is so little tonal variation in *Men in Battle* that the final effect is to make everything Bessie reports seem dull and routine. The really impressive quality of the book is its accumulation of detail into what seems to be a truly objective record of the final months of the International Brigades. It is this factual quality which makes the book's heartbreaking bitterness so convincing.

One of the interesting elements in *Men in Battle* is that in its early chapters it bears considerable resemblance to *Volunteer in Spain*. Like Sommerfield, Bessie and the others in his group travel through France on their way to Spain, feeling the same exhilaration and the same nervousness that the early volunteers had felt two years before. Their actual entrance into Spain is more difficult, since they have to cross the Pyrenees on foot instead of making the relatively easy sea voyage, but the excitement of finally arriving on Spanish soil is very much the same. Only when Bessie tells of being assigned to duty does the real difference between the two experiences become clear to the reader.

After a brief period of training, Bessie is sent as a replacement to the Fifteenth International Brigade, being reconstituted after a disastrous retreat from Belchite. Bessie and the men he is with are nervous, fearful of battle but anxious to get into it, and still excited about the war. The veterans they join near the front are sick, angry, and disgusted. The encounter between the two groups is the classic confrontation of rookie and old soldier:

Here was apparent total demoralization, utter fatigue, rampant individualism. The men criticized their command mercilessly; it sounded like treason to us . . . They barked at each other and at us; they cursed continuously, making accusations that horrified the new replacements . . . Irving N — was shocked, but not beyond speech.

"Comrades," he said. "Do I understand you retreated and threw your guns away?"

"Yeh," they said.

"But comrades," he said, "that's cowardice. Don't you realize how difficult it is for the government to get arms? Don't you realize that unless we lick Fascism all over the world it won't be long before — "

"Shit," some one said; they looked at him and spat. I expected them to tear him to pieces.[10]

Not all the effusions of Sommerfield, the militant editorials in the *Daily Worker,* or the impassioned speeches of André Marty or Pasionaria would ever make war seem romantic again to men like these.

The war that Bessie knew had little of romance in it. In his first action with the Fifteenth Brigade he was part of a disorderly retreat. In company with some others, he plunged headlong through a hidden camp occupied by some Moors fighting with the Insurgents, and in the wild confusion somehow escaped. (pp. 117–19) He describes whole nights and days under fire, and the hopeless experience of being bombed and knowing

[10] Bessie, *Men in Battle*, pp. 83–84. Subsequent references will be incorporated in the text.

that the enemy can bomb you whenever he wishes, since your side no longer has any air force worth mentioning.

It is a hard war, and it leads Bessie to ponder the motives of the men who are fighting it. If his thoughts on the subject are not entirely lucid, they at least represent a desire to understand rather than to accept stock answers:

Men went to Spain for various reasons, but behind almost every man I met there was a common restlessness, a loneliness. In action these men would fight like devils, with the desperation of an iron-bound conscience; in private conversation there was something else again. I know, about myself, that the historical event of Spain had coincided with a long-felt compulsion to complete the destruction of the training I had received all through my youth. There were two major reasons for my being there: to achieve self-integration, and to lend my individual strength (such as it was) to the fight against our eternal enemy — oppression; and the validity of the second reason was not impaired by the fact that it was a shade weaker than the first. (pp. 181–82)

The idea that war can be a means to self-integration appears also in Sommerfield's book, but in a different guise; there it is romanticized, here it is simply acknowledged as a force.

The subject reappears later in *Men in Battle*. During a lull in the fighting, Bessie thinks of the differences between what war means to the men in the lines and what it means to those they are fighting for. Other writers of the Spanish Civil War have said or implied that everyone is engaged in the war: the propagandist, the party leader, and the moneyraiser as much as the soldier. The notion is common to literature written by civilians about all wars: it is an attempt to rationalize their nonparticipation in the fighting. Bessie does more than deny this pleasant fiction; he denies that there is any connection between the soldier and the others. In spite of this chasm separating the realms of experience, the soldier can think of love,

and it is only through love that the terrible suffering of war
can be justified:

For it is love alone that can, for even a moment of our time, give you
the illusion that you are not alone, penetrate your loneliness and separate it from you for that moment. And you are afraid that you will
die without that love; you are not just afraid to *die*. And this is the
meaning of it all (the people's war) ; these men behind the fragile
rocks, these men whose tender flesh is torn to pieces by the hot and
ragged steel; they could not accept their death with such good grace
if they did not love so deeply and so well — were not determined that
love must come alive in the world. What other reason could there be
for dying? What other reason for this blood on your hands? (pp.
291–92)

The perspective of time makes these last questions poignant.
It would be more than difficult to show that the Spanish Civil
War, or any of the other great and small conflicts since, brought
love alive into the world, and we are forced to conclude that
on these grounds the agony *was* in vain, that the dying and
the bloody hands proved nothing and changed nothing. More
important, such a passage shows how far the Spanish experience could drive men from their original impulses and beliefs.
The dream of the rise of the proletariat, of the necessity for
eliminating the enemies of the people, of the "welded front"
of workers and soldiers fighting against a "fascist monster,
slimed from the night," has in this case come to be indistinguishable from the Christian dream of love: the true Soviet
seems to have become the City of God.

Reading *Men in Battle* today, we have the strong conviction
that Bessie knew how futile the dream was to prove, for the
book is in no way optimistic. The details of Bessie's experiences are presented with painstaking honesty, as if this war
and its conditions had made rhetoric and heroic postures impossible. The one note in the book which might be called

sentimental — the letters written by Bessie to his sons and his sons' answers — is unobtrusive, and it adds depth to our picture of the author. Otherwise, he is an objective recorder of action and his own emotions. He makes no attempt to hide the continual fear and discomfort he experienced as a front-line soldier, nor to explain away as "contributing to the greater good" his ultimately successful attempt to get a safer billet behind the lines. He writes also of the cowards and the deserters in the Brigades, and he describes the troubles between Spaniards and foreigners in the Fifteenth Brigade. All were part of the war he saw.

The honesty of *Men in Battle* underlines the difference between the war Bessie records in this memoir and the war he invents in his later novel, *The Un-Americans*. The novel is not surprising when we consider Bessie's years as a member of the Communist party, his experience as a film writer and as one of the Hollywood Ten, and his subsequent years of marginal existence as an outcast in the United States. The novel is clearly intended to be his answer to and revenge upon those who have scorned his belief or betrayed it, and they are legion. Among the targets of his wrath (apart from the most obvious, the House Committee on Un-American Activities) are a newsman who is a caricature of all the reporters-turned-pundit, a writer who represents Ernest Hemingway, psychiatry, the American judicial system, Franklin Delano Roosevelt, the publishing business, and the apostates from the true faith whose defection is accompanied by a complete dissolution of moral integrity. At least some of these would appear to offer easy and rewarding targets for an angry satirist who has known them at first hand, even if his aim were not always deadly. But apparently too much had happened to Alvah Bessie in the years since he saw so clearly the realities of the war in Spain: he had put in some years in Hollywood, he had served a prison term, and he had passed almost two decades in the increasingly close confines of the American Communist party. In *The Un-Americans*, he is angry, baffled, and in the end pitiful.

Bessie is utterly serious about the subject of his novel. His hero, Ben Blau, is as staunch and noble and self-reliant as that earlier American individualist, Natty Bumppo. Bessie follows Blau's career from the point at which he abandons his job as a foreign correspondent to join the Loyalist Army, to a kind of resolution in an American prison ten years later. Between the two events Blau proves himself to be a first-class fighting man, both in Spain and during World War II; he joins the Communist party, having been impressed by the discipline and devotion of the party members in Spain; he serves the party so well that his first wife leaves him — he loves the party more than he loves her; he writes a book about Spain and works for the *Daily Worker*; he testifies before a Congressional committee, routing the forces of evil with his wit and ruthless logic; he goes to jail on a trumped-up charge, and there his skull is fractured by a fawning toady who is trying to curry favor with the authorities. Through it all he remains plain Ben Blau, ugly but with "a beautiful smile," friend to the common man, loyal even to those who betray him, firm and unwavering in his beliefs. If the political climate in this country ever changed sufficiently, we might see him played on the screen by Gregory Peck or Rock Hudson.

That Blau's virtues may shine the more clearly, Bessie provides a deep-dyed villain named Francis Xavier Lang. As a correspondent in Spain, Lang is a firm supporter of the Loyalists, he is in love with a beautiful government official who is an agit-prop expert, and he is a great admirer of La Pasionaria. But because he refuses to accept reality, he cannot understand Blau's decision to join the Loyalist army. The similarity between Lang's relationship with Blau and Vincent Sheean's relationship with Jim Lardner is almost certainly intentional. Later on, Lang has great success as a lecturer and writer; briefly and secretly he is a member of the party, but he leaves without hesitation when asked to do so by his good friend, FDR. Eventually he is the chief government witness in the rigged trial of Ben Blau. Lang is a drunkard, a compulsive Don Juan who is ultimately stimulated only by perversion (Blau, of course, is loyal to his women and likes his sex straight, with no bourgeois frills). He tries to come to terms with his guilty conscience through psychoanalysis (another bourgeois frill), but of course this does him little good, and his analyst passes his confidences on to the FBI. Blau, as we might expect, forgives Lang all his sins.

There is no doubt that Bessie's Spanish experience helped shape his later career, or that it assumed increasing importance in his mind. No other events described in *The Un-Americans* have quite the same glow; only in the Loyalist army did Blau find true happiness and the kind of "integration" that is so important in Hemingway's *For Whom the Bell Tolls*. For Bessie, the Spanish War is kind of an Edenic past, a paradise of solidarity from which Blau is cast out by the forces of evil and to which he can never return.

The Un-Americans is told in a series of flashbacks, and the war in Spain recurs time and again. In a book that is largely about communism in this century, there is little or no important mention of Marx, Engels, Lenin, Stalin, Duclos, Togliatti, Harry Pollitt, Earl Browder, or William Z. Foster. The heroic figure out of history is La Pasionaria, whose appeal for American writers (except, of course, Hemingway) was very great. Lang, even in the testimony which betrays Blau, speaks of her as "one of the greatest human beings of our generation, one of the greatest leaders of her people ever to have emerged upon the stage of history. . . ."[11] The novel contains a long description of a Communist party meeting in Spain, at which Pasionaria controls a wildly enthusiastic crowd with her impassioned oratory. (pp. 70–82) The novel's most emotional scene describes the departure of the foreign volunteers from Spain, with a parade and another impassioned speech by Pasionaria. (pp. 136–37) In all of this there is a note of desperate nostalgia; for Blau and his creator the years after 1938 brought no moments to match these.

It cannot be easy for a man to have his real life end so early, and in further extenuation of Bessie it ought to be pointed out that the two institutions he refrains from attacking in *The Un-Americans*, the movie industry and the Communist party, were not especially kind to him. The greatest damage they did to him was to help ruin him as a writer, damage which is shown only too clearly by a comparison of *Men in Battle* and *The Un-Americans*. The important virtue of the earlier book was its honesty; the writing gave no sign that Bessie would ever be a writer of great importance, but he seemed at the time to have an ability to deal with unpleasant experience and unpalatable truths without cant. Even at its most plodding, *Men in Battle* is impressively free of pretension and sugar-coating.

But Bessie's perceptions were dulled over the years by the experience of writing for the screen and of belonging to a political group whose natural tendency to see men and events in absolute terms was exacerbated by unpopularity and persecution. There are no shadings in *The Un-Americans*: a Communist is a good man, a liberal a bad man, a conservative a Fascist, a man without politics a fool and a knave. The courtroom scene in which Blau vanquishes his tormentors is the

[11] Alvah Bessie, *The Un-Americans* (London: John Calder, 1957), p. 11. Subsequent references will be incorporated in the text.

rawest melodrama. There is even the equivalent of the final Hollywood fadeout with the hero and heroine walking hand in hand into the sunset; from his prison bed Blau writes the woman who had stood by him through all his sufferings to say that at last he can accept her love because he has come to realize that it will enforce the love he feels for the people and expresses through the party. Hardly a cliché of movie-making is omitted from the novel.

Many people have regarded the attraction exerted by Hollywood upon Communist writers as hilarious. There *is* something funny about the spectacle of men who profess their dedication to a classless society and the dictatorship of the proletariat living in and off of the most notorious center of conspicuous waste in our society, and wasting with the best while observing punctiliously the niceties of our most rigidly stratified industry. Those who have taken the trouble to investigate this relationship further are even more amused by the fact that the Communist screen writers in their heyday seem to have written mostly gangster pictures, musical comedies, and, during World War II, recruiting films like *Destination Tokyo, The Pride of the Marines,* and *Cloak and Dagger.*[12] But this is not just amusing. It is perfectly natural, and it seems unlikely that the screen writers were as unhappy with their work as they are commonly assumed to have been, and as they have sometimes claimed. For men who had already accepted a view of the world which made absolute and permanent distinctions between good and bad in the name of historical necessity, it cannot have seemed too difficult to write scenarios which made the same distinctions, if on different grounds. The resemblance between *The Un-Americans* and Hollywood's typical drama has already been noted; the resemblance of that novel to such "proletarian" novels of the thirties as *March-*

[12] Kempton, *Part of Our Time,* pp. 193–200.

ing! Marching! is also remarkably close. For the Communist artist outside New York's lower East Side, Hollywood had definite attractions as a home away from home.

Alvah Bessie's immediate response to his experiences in Spain was not unlike Stephen Spender's. Both men, in writing about Spain during the war or immediately after its close, were concerned with recording their horror at what they had seen or experienced. In *Men in Battle*, as in Spender's poems, political ideas fade into the background before the overwhelming fact of human suffering and the tragedy of defeat. Earlier, a comparison was made between Bessie's book and John Sommerfield's *Volunteer in Spain*; a comparison of the conclusions of the two books is also instructive. Sommerfield ends his narrative with a picture of war's horror, and then appends a chapter in which he tries to use political emotionalism to explain away the horror. At the end of Bessie's book the Internationals are being withdrawn from the fighting, preparatory to being sent home:

. . . We were jittery, and the truck moved slowly down the long ramp toward the bridge, and slowly across the narrow, sounding planks. To your right was the collapsed skeleton of the old bridge that we had blown up to cover our retreat last April; it lay half in and half out of the water, like a wrecked dirigible. The farther shore was pitted with enormous craters left by the bombing that had been going on every day for two months now. We moved off the bridge and up-grade into the twin-town, Mora La Nueva, and I looked back at the yellow Ebro before we turned the corner. It was wide and placid in the brilliant sun; its surface shimmered with a million broken flecks of quiet light. I thought of Aaron. (p. 345)

The possibilities for an "up-beat" ending are here. There is the image of the placid river, amidst all the destruction, which could have been compared to the flow of history; the memory of the dead friend could have been turned into a sermon on the better world the dead had helped usher in, as Sommerfield did with John Cornford. But the book ends here. Aaron is dead and the war lost, and there is nothing more to say.

While Sommerfield left Spain early enough to avoid disillusion, and Spender turned from politics to an exclusive concern (in his poetry at least) with private events and private emotions, Bessie in later years somehow managed to reconstitute his earlier beliefs, almost as if the war had never happened, except that, as *The Un-Americans* demonstrates, it remained for him a central event. Viewed from his own angle, Bessie's experience in Spain as recorded in *Men in Battle* might seem to have been a period of disease, and the record itself an error which the later novel atoned for. Whatever Bessie's later experience may have been, it does not change *Men in Battle*, which remains a book demonstrating vividly the way in which prolonged exposure to violence can turn idealism into ashes, and which shows that when no sacrifice will suffice, any slogan or dogma is irrelevant. For the duration of the time he took to write *Men in Battle*, at least, Bessie abandoned the tired abstractions and simply recorded an experience of desolation and defeat.

This desolation is also at the heart of three very different novels dealing with the Spanish War: Robert Payne's *The Song of the Peasant*, John Dos Passos' *Adventures of a Young Man*, and Humphrey Slater's *The Heretics*. Payne was one of the very few non-Spanish writers courageous enough to deal with the Spanish War in terms of Spanish characters, and the only one to give expression to the disillusion caused by the war among the Spanish peasants. His novel[13] is set in a Catalan fishing village during the years 1935 to 1939. In the early part of the novel, Payne's primary purpose is to evoke the atmos-

[13] (London: William Heinemann, 1939.) Page references incorporated in the text.

phere of the village by showing us the lives of the fishermen and their close communion with nature. The early narrative is broken by extended and impassioned descriptions of the Catalan countryside and of the fishermen at work on the sea. The contrast between the natural lives of the villagers and the unnatural events of the war is made clear when the first mention of the war is followed almost immediately by a long rhapsodic passage in which a woman gives birth to a child in an ecstatic communion with nature. The outbreak of war is an unnatural birth, involving the violation of nature, in direct antithesis to the natural birth of the child, in which human and nonhuman become one. (pp. 139–51)

Payne's peasants, unlike the noble savages of Elliott Paul's *The Life and Death of a Spanish Town,* are highly sophisticated in their politics, and in describing their existence before the war, Payne makes it clear that politics was an important part of their lives. The most important characters in *The Song of the Peasant* are Pere Campo, an Anarchist and the leader of the fishermen's cooperative, and Tomas Mora, a Communist stonemason who has as little patience with anarchism as had Robert Jordan: "I have this against the anarchists — dynamite. It's useless. Dynamite is a sort of symbol of your suicidal tendencies — a beautiful death and to hell with everyone! It's not enough." (p. 91) Despite their differences, Campo and Mora are in fundamental opposition to the village priest, who defines his position in a defense of the right-wing government which held power before the elections of February, 1936: ". . . I beg you to discard impious thoughts and never allow yourselves to think evilly of the State which is also a representative pattern, not only of Christ but of Christianity. . . ." (p. 98) Such an attitude permits Campo and Mora to suppress their own differences and join in a common cause.

Having established the peasants' communion with nature

and their consciousness of the political realities, Payne concludes the first section of the novel with the events of the early days of the Civil War. Campo and other villagers go off to Barcelona to join in the fighting there, and help to put down the revolt of the military. The ecstatic tone of the earlier descriptions of the natural world is abandoned here for reportorial accounts of the bloody fighting. The change in tone is noticeable, but it does not really jar the reader until the conclusion of this first section, the announcement of the death of Durruti. This famous Anarchist leader, a key figure in the Barcelona fighting, had led a column to help in the defense of Madrid. In the pages of this novel, as in history, Durruti was a natural leader, and his death signals the end of the first days of the war, when the whole thing seemed to be a wonderful and charming adventure.

Two years elapse before the narrative is resumed; the second part of the novel focuses on the campaigns around the Ebro River, in which Alvah Bessie also participated. Mora and Campo are now in the army, and both suffer through the defeat of the Loyalists. The elements of the narrative here achieve a closer integration than in the first section of the novel. The battle scenes are sharper and more personal than the earlier scenes in Barcelona, which on occasion read like communiqués; the evocations of nature which disturbed the flow of narrative in the first section are here made an integral part of the experience of the characters. Man and nature are no longer close; Mora and Campo are removed from the life of the village, and while nature is not hostile (the pathetic fallacy is not involved here) the men no longer feel comfortable with it. The natural setting reflects the ravages of war, and in their dislocation the two men are no longer able to rely on it, any more than they can rely on other humans. At the end, Campo is dead, and Mora is himself wounded. He returns to the village to direct its government, arriving in time to witness its total destruction in an air raid. Mora is left alone in a wasteland, his friends dead, his village a ruin, his cause lost.

Like the other literature under consideration in this chapter, *The Song of the Peasant* offers no consolation to its characters or to its readers. The destruction caused by the war is in the end pointless because the cause in whose name the war was waged has been lost. As in Bessie's memoir and Spender's poetry, *The Song of the Peasant* contains no direct condemnation of politics or political action, no attempt to put the blame for all this destruction on parties or dogmas. Instead, politics simply fade into insignificance beside the enormity of the degradations men are prepared to visit on one another and upon nature. Payne does not choose between the political ideologies of Mora and Campo; in fact, apart from his evident sympathy for the Loyalists, he is not much concerned with ideology. He makes clear, however, that both of his heroes are motivated by political concepts, and that neither anarchism nor communism is capable of sustaining its believers in a world whose only law is violence. To the men who hold them, such beliefs may seem worth fighting for, but in the end they are incapable of explaining or even ameliorating the disasters of the war.

There are a number of other writers in whose work the problems of politics are treated more directly, and in which politics is seen as one of the forces which cause disillusion. John Dos Passos, for example, had gone a long way down the road toward disaffection with left-wing politics before the Spanish Civil War broke out, and he was convinced that neither communism nor any other radical political or economic program could correct the weaknesses of our system. At the same time, he had long been sympathetic with radical causes, and when the war broke out in Spain he went there in the hope that he might find that for once all men of good will could work together, that Communist, Socialist, and liberal together could save Spain from Franco and his Italian and German allies. The conditions of the war itself and Dos Passos' own attitude foreordained his further disappointment.

Dos Passos, it seems clear, went to Spain prepared to blame the Communist party for whatever faults he might find, and he was to find many. This is not to say that he did not undergo experiences which would have embittered anyone. Josephine Herbst, in her fine memoir, "The Starched Blue Sky of Spain," has recorded a chilling episode in which Dos Passos sought to find the whereabouts of an old Spanish friend. Hemingway tried to dissuade him, "because Dos was conspicuously making inquiries and might get everybody into trouble if he persisted."[14] It develops that the man had already been shot as a spy, and in the end Hemingway undertook to tell this to Dos Passos. But the latter did not believe that his old friend had in fact been a spy, nor, for that matter, did Miss Herbst. Such an arbitrary exercise of power would have aroused the suspicion of anyone more sophisticated than was Hemingway at the time, and it unquestionably had its effect upon Dos Passos.

This incident and others like it help to account for the fact that Dos Passos tended to put all of the blame for the Loyalists' difficulties on the Communists:

The communists in Spain fought well against the fascists, but they also fought against the syndicalists, the socialists who made up the bulk of organized labor and against the middleclass liberals of Catalonia and the Basque country. These were the elements from which the Republic was born . . . In the end their war against Spanish

[14] *The Noble Savage*, I (March, 1960), p. 93.

independence did as much as Franco's superior military skill to sap the republican will to resist.[15]

This comment deserves some attention because, justified as his animosity unquestionably was, Dos Passos' analysis is almost certainly inaccurate. The Communists in Spain did fight with their allies, but not with the socialists or the middle-class liberals of Catalonia and the Basque country. In fact, as a number of reputable historians have shown, the Communists made common cause with these groups in order to diminish the power of the more radical anarchists and the anti-Stalinist Marxists of the POUM. Further, it is doubtful that Communist activities sapped "the republican will to resist" to any crucial extent. Even George Orwell, who suffered personally as a result of these activities, admits that the kind of unified command demanded by the Communists was probably essential to successful military action. In any case, the Loyalists' internal weaknesses were the result of years of internal strife, for which the Communists were by no means solely responsible, and it is clear that the real handicap under which the Loyalists struggled was the lack of assistance from France, Great Britain, and the United States, for which the Communists can hardly be blamed. Finally, as Robert Colodny's *The Struggle for Madrid* and Hugh Thomas' *The Spanish Civil War* have both shown, Franco's advantage lay in his abundance of trained soldiers and the assistance he received from Hitler's Germany and Mussolini's Italy, not in any supposed strategic superiority. As Colodny points out, even a moderately adept strategist could have taken Madrid for the Insurgents in 1936 and could almost certainly have ended the war in a few months.

The point of all this is that Dos Passos wrote about his Spanish experience from a special point of view, and that his

[15] John Dos Passos, *The Theme Is Freedom* (New York: Dodd, Mead, 1956), p. 118.

novel, *The Adventures of a Young Man*,[16] derives as much from his own disillusion with communism and its agents as from what he actually saw in Spain. Most of the action of the novel takes place in the United States, in the mill and mining towns whose strikes and riots attracted Dos Passos' sympathetic attention during the thirties, and in New York, where the traditional bohemianism of Greenwich Village became for a while almost indistinguishable from radical activism. But the story of Dos Passos' hero, Glen Spotswood, comes to its inevitable conclusion in Spain.

Arthur Koestler once described in barbed terms the *curriculum vitae* of a typical European radical during the thirties:

1930–3: unemployment and living on the dole;
1933–5: concentration camp in Germany;
1935–6: unemployment in France, but no dole;
1936–9: volunteer in Spain, twice wounded, the second time in the lung;
1939–?: concentration camp in France.[17]

Glen Spotswood's activities form a similarly typical curriculum for young American radicals of the same generation. His story includes a lower middle-class upbringing, exposure to Marxism through a teacher or an old radical, mass meetings in New York or Chicago, strikes in which the strikers are betrayed and beaten by their own leaders, disillusion with the Communist party, the formation of an independent and short-lived Marxist organization, and the eventual trip to Spain. The journey ended for a good many, as it did for Glen Spotswood, with a messy and meaningless death on a Spanish hillside. It had too often included a good deal of hunger and misery, a jail term or two, and a few wild moments of hope.

[16] (New York: Harcourt, Brace, 1937.) Page references incorporated in the text.
[17] *The Scum of the Earth* (New York: Macmillan Co., 1941), pp. 120–21.

Spotswood's Spanish experience can be quickly described. He comes to Spain at the end of his hopes; he has exhausted the possibilities of radical activity in the United States, and although bitter, he has not lost hope that he can be useful somewhere. After an arduous trip across the Pyrenees into Spain he has a moment of pure happiness, because he believes that he is at last present in a place where right and wrong confront each other. A little later he has another good moment when he meets a Spaniard who had been his friend during a strike in the United States. But Spain is no Armageddon for Spotswood. He is warned to stay away from his friend, an anarchist who is looked upon as a Fascist spy; later on he is informed that the friend has been shot. The resemblance to Dos Passos' own experience in connection with his friend Robles is obvious. Spotswood meets another friend of long standing who is now commander of a battalion; this friend, suspicious because Spotswood had been dismissed from the party, accuses him of being a fifth columnist and arranges for him to be stuck behind the lines in a meaningless and menial job. (pp. 307–10) In the end, Spotswood is arrested and questioned by three party authorities (one of them yet another friend) who regard as treason his failure to commit himself utterly to the party. He is imprisoned and only released to be sent on a desperate and futile errand which inevitably ends in his death. (pp. 315–22)

Adventures of a Young Man is Dos Passos' farewell to the radical movement and his explanation of his reasons for departing. He was to go on from this point to an interest in the early days of the United States, a period whose ideals he believed had been betrayed, and he has come to rest recently in the company of William Buckley and the group for which the *National Review* is home. In this trip through the political spectrum, so typical of our times, he does not seem to have lost his sympathy for the truly downtrodden. In this sense, he was still in 1939 the same writer who had grown so impassioned over the fates of Sacco and Vanzetti, and who had written after their execution, "All right; we are two countries." By 1939 he had, as he has written, "rejoined the United States,"[18] and he had long since dissociated himself from the Communist party, but he was still as angry at the treatment of the oppressed in *Adventures of a Young Man* as he had been at the plight of the miners in Harlan County or the industrial workers in Detroit in 1932.

What changed in the intervening years was the literary effect of his anger; in *USA* it was directed outward, with a cutting edge that revealed a sick society and showed at least some warmth for those who were trying to cure it. In *Adventures of a Young Man* the anger is gall; the society is no less sick, but social maladies have become less important than the author's bitterness at those who had been his allies, and who he feels have betrayed him. The betrayal was real enough, and in 1939 the revelation of this betrayal was still important, but after two decades the novel is as stale as the poems of Jack Lindsay or the heroics of *The Fifth Column*. All of its characters, including Glen Spotswood, are cardboard images, and the villains are no more human than Lindsay's "fascist monsters, slimed from the night." At the same time, *Adventures of a Young Man* demonstrates clearly the disillusionment with political ideas which became more common as the war in Spain continued. As the bitterness of the Loyalist defeat grew, so did the bitterness of those who felt that the defeat was caused, or at least contributed to, by those who fought on the Loyalist side but who insisted on having their own way in the prosecution of the war.

A more interesting and more rewarding book than Dos

[18] *The Theme Is Freedom*, p. 103.

Passos', Humphrey Slater's *The Heretics*,[19] develops the same idea, and Slater's target is once again the Communist party. One significant difference between the two novels resides in the fact that Dos Passos' antipathy toward the Communist party had its source outside Spain, so that his novel deals largely with events preceding the war. Slater, on the other hand, was a member of the Communist party who rose to the rank of Commissar of the Fifteenth Brigade,[20] but who renounced the party because of his experience in Spain, and who denounced it bitterly in *The Heretics* and other books written after the end of World War II.

The Heretics is interesting not only for what it says about Spain but for its method. *The Heretics* is in fact two related short novels about two very different times; Slater attempts to draw parallels between widely separated historical events by putting into his narratives of these events two sets of characters with identical names. The first part of the novel deals with the Children's Crusade, that astounding blot on the record of militant Christianity, and does not directly concern us here; the second part deals with the Spanish Civil War. Wisely, the author has not attempted to make the two sections too closely parallel, nor does he make the characters in the second part similar to those in the first except in name. Both sections, however, illustrate a single theme: heresy and dissent, whether religious or political, are natural to the intelligent and sensitive, but they will always be sought out and punished by those in control of authoritarian societies. The political orthodoxies of our time are no more tolerant or flexible than was the religious orthodoxy of the Middle Ages.

The theme is worked out in the actions of four characters, one of whom becomes an agent of the group in power and

[19] (New York: Harcourt, Brace, 1947.) Page references incorporated in the text.

[20] Thomas, *The Spanish Civil War*, p. 508.

helps destroy the others. Three of the characters, in the section dealing with the war in Spain, are English scientists, working on an anthropological experiment when the war breaks out. The two men, Simon and Paul, join different militia units as soon as they can; the latter's sister, Elizabeth, eventually becomes the mistress of Colonel Cordova, one of the few regular army officers to remain loyal to the government.

In this novel, the Loyalist government is presented as being under the domination of the Communists and the agents of the Soviet Union; the Communists are depicted as the most rigid of the political groups on the Loyalist side, able to have their way because they control the distribution of arms sent by the Soviet Union — as, in fact, was the case. Cordova is the first of the characters to feel the pinch of oppression. He serves on a high strategy board composed of three Spaniards and three Russians. The board makes decisions, over Cordova's protests, which will result in military disaster for the Republic, but which can be used in propaganda and which will also tighten the political dominance of the Communist party. (pp. 139–43) A little later, Cordova barely escapes from a trap which would have made him seem to be responsible for the very disaster he had tried to prevent, and which would have been used to prove him either an incompetent or a traitor. (pp. 152–54)

Slater shifts the reader's attention back and forth, in this part of the novel, between Cordova, Elizabeth, and Simon. Elizabeth is not simply a kept woman; she writes magazine articles and travels around the country on junkets arranged for the press. Simon serves in the front lines, but while Slater does describe some of the fighting, he is more interested in the political maneuvering that goes on even at the front. Simon becomes more and more a trusted aide of the Communist political commissars, and after the disastrous battle Cordova had tried to avoid, Simon helps his superiors convince the men that the most important problem they must face is not the stupidity of the leadership which led them into the battle but the effect of Trotskyist diversionism on their morale. (pp. 164–67) The battle as Slater describes it was stupid and wasteful; the meeting of the troops is a frightening record of the way in which skillful political leaders can turn the attention of men away from the evident facts by scaring them with an imaginary bugaboo. Slater obviously knew the technique well.

In the course of the novel the individual characters grow weaker and weaker in their relationships with an increasingly powerful government. Paul, Elizabeth's brother, had joined the "wrong" militia, just as George Orwell did in actuality, and is eventually forced into hiding and reported killed in action. When Elizabeth finds him alive she is able to smuggle him to Barcelona and with Cordova's help to arrange his escape from the country, but at the last moment Paul is captured by the secret police and is later executed. Cordova's power steadily declines. Simon goes over completely to the Communist party and goes to work as a member of the SIM (*Servicio Informacion Militar*), an especially sinister organization which bears profound resemblances to the NKVD. Simon has thus surrendered his independence and his manhood, and has become a mere agent of the state. At the end of the novel Paul is dead and Cordova is in exile in Mexico. Elizabeth is in France, dispiritedly caring for refugee children for lack of anything else to do while she awaits the birth of Cordova's child. Simon is with her, asking that she marry him, but he makes a slip which reveals his connection with the SIM; we further learn that it was Simon who betrayed Paul in Barcelona and made Paul's death inevitable.

Slater succeeds in this novel in showing the impotence of the individual in conflict with a powerful orthodoxy, and in showing that in such a conflict the orthodoxy always triumphs. Paul, Elizabeth, and Cordova are all destroyed because, in their different ways, they opposed those in control. Paul did so involuntarily, because the military unit of which he was a part was sponsored by a politically suspect group, a group for which Paul as an individual had no particular admiration. Elizabeth acts in opposition to the regime out of simple sisterly affection, Cordova out of his knowledge of war. Simon conforms to the orthodoxy and thus surrenders his existence as a human being in his willingness to ignore values and personal relationships on the orders of those in power. *The Heretics* shows more clearly than any other novel of the Spanish War the specific effects of a rigid ideology on those who are exposed to it.

The novel has its weaknesses. Simon's actions after he joins the SIM are understandable enough, but Slater fails to show us enough of Simon in the early pages to account for his willingness to accept the party's discipline. We must simply infer that he is more prone than the others to accept the idea of an impersonal history as the explanation and excuse for every kind of degradation, but we do not know why this should be so. And Simon is not the only character who is not studied thoroughly enough; the children in the first section of *The Heretics* are more fully realized than the adults of the second section, although the latter is much longer. This can be explained, of course, by the fact that Slater was much more familiar with the events he describes in the second section, and therefore devotes more attention to the events themselves than to the people involved in them. Such an explanation, however, does not make the characters more real.

In spite of the problems of character portrayal, *The Heretics* is a generally successful fictional treatment of the war, and its attitude toward the Communist party as the dominant

force in the Loyalist government gains credence because of
the author's personal experience as a high-ranking agent of
the party in Spain. The ending of the novel is bleak, but Slater
avoids the unfocused bitterness of *The Song of the Peasant*
as well as the note of personal pique which weakens *Adventures of a Young Man.* Slater makes perfectly clear his dislike
of the Communist party's activities in Spain, but the first section and his treatment of individual characters throughout
the book show that he regarded communism as only one of
many monolithic ideologies. The enemy in *The Heretics* is
not communism but orthodoxy.

Other writers were as bitter as those I have been discussing,
and as lacking in hope. The lives of these disillusioned men
have been very dissimilar, in the years since the end of the
Spanish War. Spender has been true to his resolve to keep
political matters out of his poetry, to use his verse only as a
medium for expressing private emotions. His lyric gift has
not deserted him, but some of the fire has gone out of his
poetry. His withdrawal is less common than the responses of
Bessie, Dos Passos, and Slater. All in fact have remained committed to politics, to the notion that politics is the decisive
element in our lives. Their ways have, of course, been different. Bessie has remained the dedicated servant of the Communist party. Dos Passos has gone to the other extreme, finding his most sympathetic audience among the intellectuals of
reaction. Slater, after World War II, wrote thrillers in which
the agents of the Kremlin sought to subvert Englishmen. Less
dogmatic than either Bessie or Dos Passos, he shared with
them an apparent inability to move beyond the initial response
to the hard lesson of the thirties, for which the Spanish Civil
War was the final examination room.

Spender, Bessie, Dos Passos, Payne, and Slater are by no
means unique. Their response to the experience of the Spanish

Civil War, in fact, helps to relate that conflict to every other war in which intelligent men have been forced to the understanding that belief is at the mercy of fact. Violence and betrayal cannot indefinitely, for most men of intelligence, be kept separate from the ideals for which they are used, and we do not need the literature of the Spanish Civil War to tell us this. It is nevertheless important that we see that for these men the shibboleths of twentieth-century politics, held as articles of faith for a time, simply disappear when the man becomes conscious that he can no longer accept them. Rolfe and Cornford might be dismayed by their experiences, but they responded by clinging the more fiercely to their beliefs. Spender and the others abandoned those beliefs.

6. Voyage and Exile

THE WRITERS so far discussed have shown, within the groups to which they belong, certain common characteristics. Writers like Sommerfield, Paul, and Rolfe were forced to try to convince themselves that the facts of violence with which they were confronted had no relevance to their political beliefs. That they recognized violence as ugly and destructive distinguishes them from such a man as Jack Lindsay, but the fissure between them is not wide. Lindsay (like his more famous counterpart on the other side of the trenches, Roy Campbell) could ignore violence, or glory in it, but his message is not essentially different from that of Edwin Rolfe in "City of Anguish." The horrors which Rolfe describes have no relevance (for the poet) to what he says and thinks about La Pasionaria. The same problem remains unanswered in *For Whom the Bell Tolls*. Robert Jordan never satisfactorily answers the questions raised by Anselmo, and the problems of ideology and violence are therefore unresolved.

The other variety of stock response was that manifested in Spender's poems and in a novel like *The Song of the Peasant*.

The facts of violence were accepted as final by these writers. The war was a disaster of such proportions as to be incomprehensible to the human mind, and therefore the author was justified in assuming an impenetrable pessimism. From one perspective, such an attitude looks naïve to inhabitants of a world which lives constantly with the threat of world-wide destruction, and which has learned to regard the mass deaths by bombings and gas and starvation of World War II as small potatoes. We know now that the war in Spain was a small war, and not (on our more modern scale) a fearfully destructive one. From another perspective, of course, the attitude reflected in "To a Spanish Poet" or in *The Heretics* is entirely modern. Naïveté is the characteristic we ascribe to those who failed to see that the violence which began in Spain would eventually bring us to the brink over which we may slide at any time.

In any case, a small group of writers did not make the stock responses to the war in Spain, and they have left us with most of the few real works of art which came out of that struggle. These writers are in no sense a group, nor is there much similarity in the attitudes they took toward the war. Some of them died in Spain; others fought there and survived; still others had no firsthand knowledge whatever of the war. What they share is less common experience or attitude than the ability to put the events of the war in some kind of perspective, to objectify the violent experience (real or imaginary) so that what emerges is neither confusion nor terror nor blind reverence for a god or gods but an ability to face experience and understand it without being destroyed by it. The spirit of these men is perhaps most characteristically expressed in a poem by a young American who died in Spain. It is the poem of a very young man, and it lacks technical polish, but it acknowledges that war is grim without being deranged by the knowledge:

> Comrades, the battle is bloody and the war is long;
> Still let us climb the gray hill and charge the guns,
> Pressing with lean bayonets towards the slope beyond.
> Soon those who are still living will see the green grass,
> A free bright country shining with a star;
> And those who charge the guns will be remembered,
> And from red blood white pinnacles will tower.[1]

The writers who surmounted the problem and created something like pinnacles out of the red blood of the Spanish War include the poets Cecil Day Lewis, George Barker, and Charles Donnelly; Ernest Hemingway in one brief story, "Old Man at the Bridge"; and George Orwell. The works upon which this judgment is based, and with which this chapter is concerned, may not be masterpieces, but they all demonstrate the possibility of creating literature out of violence, even when that violence is not fully understood. In these few works, the authors have gone beyond the immediate sensation of terror which gives rise to such a poem as "To a Spanish Poet"; they have also avoided the bleak pessimism of *Song of the Peasant*. Terror is certainly part of the emotional weight of such works, and none of them is optimistic, but their authors are not confined by either terror or negation.

The poems of the British writer C. Day Lewis provide an instructive example of the way in which different attitudes were rendered by the same person. Lewis wrote a number of poems about the war in Spain which were later included in his volume *Overtures to Death*, a collection which represented his farewell to the poetry of politics. The reasons for Day Lewis's decision to turn toward the personal and away from

[1] Sam Levinger, quoted in Murray Kempton, *Part of Our Time*, p. 316.

politics are clear in three of the poems which deal with the
Spanish conflict.

One of these poems, "The Nabara," is entirely conventional
in its rendering of heroic Loyalists (in this case Basque fishermen) and its implicit plea for support of the Loyalist cause.
Day Lewis, who moved in the Auden orbit at Oxford and
during the middle thirties, was sympathetic with the Loyalists from the beginning, and in "The Nabara" he undertook
to create an epic out of the attempts of the Basques, cut off in
the North from the rest of Loyalist Spain, to get arms ashore
under the guns of an Insurgent cruiser. Because Day Lewis
is a genuine poet, and because the incidents he describes are
decidedly exciting, "The Nabara" carries the reader along,
and he cannot help but become involved in the struggle of the
courageous men in their little trawlers. But the moral presented at the end is too much the expected thing, too much the
celebration of heroism and the manipulation of cant abstractions:

> Freedom was more than a word, more than the base coinage
> Of politicians who hiding behind the skirts of peace
> They had defiled, gave up that country to rack and carnage;
> For whom, indelibly stamped with history's contempt,
> Remains but to haunt the blackened shell of their policies.
> For these I have told of, freedom was flesh and blood — a mortal
> Body, the gun-breech hot to its touch; yet the battle's height
> Raised it to love's meridian and held it awhile immortal;
> And its light through time still flashes like a star's that
>   has turned to ashes
> Long after Nabara's passion was quenched in the sun's heart.[2]

Technically, this is inventive poetry: rhyme is handled re-
sourcefully, the metrics bear the reader along despite a some-

[2] Cecil Day Lewis, *Collected Poems* (London: Jonathan Cape, 1954),
p. 200.

what prosaic feeling. But the language is uninspired, the imagery confused; if the images in the seventh and eighth lines have some vitality, "the blackened shell of their policies" has none at all, and "who hiding behind" is simply disastrous. This is more rational and more accomplished than the poetry of a Jack Lindsay or a Roy Campbell, but it is akin to their verse in spirit.

Day Lewis tried again in "The Volunteers," [3] and again the rather conventional sentiment of the poem tends to destroy its effectiveness. The war in Spain is seen, in this poem, as part of man's eternal struggle for freedom, echoing such a sentiment as Rex Warner's "It was us too they defended who defended Madrid." Here, the volunteers themselves speak, giving their reasons for going to Spain to fight, reasons which carry a heavy weight of self-gratulation:

> Tell them in England, if they ask
> What brought us to these wars,
> To this plateau beneath the night's
> Grave manifold of stars —
> . . . .
> We came because our open eyes
> Could see no other way.
>
> There was no other way to keep
> Man's flickering truth alight;
> These stars will witness that our course
> Burned briefer, not less bright.

There is nothing seriously wrong with this poetry; again, Day Lewis is in command of his technique, and the ballad stanza works well enough. But there is nothing especially interesting about the poem, either, unless it is the final stanza, which contains a strong (and clearly unintentional) suggestion that the

[3] *Collected Poems*, pp. 190–91.

Spanish Civil War is similar to Britain's Imperial wars, probably because the verse closely resembles Housman's "1887"[4] with the irony stripped away:

> Here in a parched and stranger place
> We fight for England free,
> The good our fathers won for her
> The land they hoped to see.

Day Lewis obviously intended this stanza to suggest no more than that the volunteers in Spain had taken up the fight for liberty, but the final lines recall the Sudan, the Boer War, the Indian wars more than any struggle for freedom within England itself. Even without the discordant suggestions of this final stanza, the poem is not especially successful.

"Bombers"[5] is a very different matter. In this poem, Day Lewis removes himself from a direct statement about the war in Spain, although the poem was clearly inspired by the bombing of civilian populations that first became important in Spain and in China after 1937. Like other poems in *Overtures to Death* which do not deal directly with Spain, "Bombers" is an expression of the poet's concern over the imminence of a

---

[4] The echo of the final stanzas of Housman's poem is especially noticeable:

> We pledge in peace by farm and town
>   The Queen they served in war,
> And fire the beacons up and down
>   The land they perished for.

> "God save the Queen" we living sing,
>   From height to height 'tis heard;
> And with the rest your voices ring,
>   Lads of the Fifty-third.

> Oh, God will save her, fear you not!
>   Be you the men you've been,
> Get you the men your fathers got,
>   And God will save the Queen.

[5] *Collected Poems*, p. 170.

general war. The militant note of "The Nabara" and "The Volunteers" is supplanted here by concern for life itself, and the abstract language of the other poems gives way to a brilliantly ironic use of natural imagery.

Through the first three stanzas of "Bombers," Day Lewis employs superficially pleasant metaphors of birth and growth, relating them to a sound whose significance is not immediately clear. That the innocent quality of these figures is a delusion begins to become clear only in the third stanza:

> Through the vague morning, the heart preoccupied,
> A deep in air buried grain of sound
> Starts and grows, as yet unwarning —
> The tremor of baited deep-sea line.
>
> Swells the seed, and now the tight sound-buds
> Vibrate, upholding their paean flowers
> To the sun. There are bees in sky-bells droning,
> Flares of crimson at the heart unfold.
>
> Children look up, and the elms spring-garlanded
> Tossing their heads and marked for the axe
> Gallant or woebegone, alike unlucky —
> Earth shakes beneath us: we imagine loss.

In the first two stanzas, only the word "unwarning" and the phrase "Flares of crimson" give any overt indication of the real import of the poem. In the third stanza the association of the watching children with the elms "marked for the axe," is a more explicit warning than anything that has gone before, and it leads to the final line of the stanza with its preparation for the clear death images of the poem's final stanzas:

> Black as vermin, crawling in echelon
> Beneath the cloud-floor, the bombers come:
> The heavy angels, carrying harm in
> Their wombs that ache to be rid of death.

This is the seed that grows for ruin,
The iron embryo conceived in fear.
Soon or late its need must be answered —
In fear delivered, and screeching fire.

Choose between your child and this fatal embryo.
Shall your guilt bear arms, and the sons you want
Be condemned to die by the powers you paid for
And haunt the houses you never built?

The image of the seed, presented first in the opening stanza, is here revived and given a darkly ironic twist in the evocative and reverberant metaphor of the bombs as iron embryos in the bomb-bay-wombs of the planes. Other images from the opening stanza are also recalled here, as innocent bees become vermin, flares of crimson become "screeching fire," and the innocent children of the third stanza are given a different reality as the sacrifices demanded by death.

If the final stanza is more abstract and less powerful than the rest of the poem, it serves a vital purpose, for it reminds the reader that the choice is his, that the machines which bring death from the sky are sent by "the powers you paid for." If Day Lewis represents violence as coming through machines, he also demonstrates an awareness that the machines neither create nor direct themselves. Death is the enemy, but it is no mere abstraction, nor is it meted out only by the "other" side. Day Lewis has gone beyond the emotional identifications he made in the earlier poems (the Insurgent cruiser as a death-dealing machine, opposed to the man-made fragility of the Basque fishing trawlers) to an expression which is entirely appropriate to the situation of the late thirties, when the seeds of world-wide violence were beginning to germinate. He has developed his poem using a series of closely related metaphors, all appropriate to his subject. The poem is pessimistic, but it is not merely pessimistic, since it suggests that the apparently inhuman violence has its sources in human behavior.

Day Lewis's important accomplishment resulted from his ability to overcome an earlier tendency to glorify the Loyalist cause in terms so abstract as to defeat his poetic purposes. "Bombers" shows the level of achievement possible to a poet of considerable natural talent when the poetic imagination is permitted to work directly on the experience of violence, when ideological assumptions are genuinely fused with poetic perception.

A different poet, George Barker, had a different kind of success. Barker, whose poems I discussed in some detail in Chapter 4, deserves at least brief mention in this context. Although his poetry was clearly intended to arouse sympathy for the Loyalists, and although it makes use of imagery at least as unusual as that in Spender's wilder poems, Barker was no mere propagandist (Spender's critical comments in *Left Review* show this), and his use of surrealistic images of destruction is more controlled and therefore more effective than Spender's. "Calamiterror" and "Elegy for Spain" deserve at least passing mention as poems which still have the power to move the reader.

More prominent mention must be made of Hemingway's one truly successful work about the Spanish Civil War, the short story "Old Man at the Bridge."[6] Originally published as one of a series of dispatches to the short-lived magazine *Ken*, this brief vignette resembles in some way Hemingway's earlier stories about the effect of modern war on civilians, for example "On the Quai at Smyrna," but it gains in effectiveness because the violence in the story is always out of sight.

[6] *The Short Stories of Ernest Hemingway* (New York: The Modern Library [n.d.]), pp. 176–78. Originally published as "The Old Man at the Bridge," *Ken*, I (May 19, 1938), p. 36.

Violence is a constant menace, and the entire motivating force of the action, but it is never brought directly into the story. "Old Man at the Bridge" is about an old man, never named, who has left his native town as part of a mass exodus before a Fascist advance. He has reached the Ebro River, but he is too tired to go any further. The Loyalist officer who narrates the story questions the old man; his whole occupation has been caring for two goats, a cat, and four pigeons, but he has to leave them behind. He is "without politics"; he refuses a ride on one of the trucks carrying refugees toward Barcelona because he knows "no one in that direction"; he is worried about the fate of the animals he has had to leave behind. There is nothing whatever to be done for him: "It was Easter Sunday and the Fascists were advancing toward the Ebro. It was a gray overcast day with a low ceiling so their planes were not up. That and the fact that cats know how to look after themselves was all the good luck that old man would ever have."[7]

The story has attracted some critical attention because it stands in such sharp contrast to Hemingway's other writings about Spain, but the critics who have mentioned it seem not to have examined it thoroughly. Edmund Wilson, for example, notes that it "outweighs the whole of *The Fifth Column* and all [Hemingway's] Spanish dispatches. . . . It is a story which takes its place among the war prints of Callot and Goya, artists whose union of elegance with sharpness has already been recalled by Hemingway in his earlier battle pieces: a story which might have been written about almost any war."[8] Alfred Kazin, another admirer of the story, gives it a more local application: "It was a record of the better things Hem-

[7] *Ibid.*, p. 178.

[8] Edmund Wilson, "Hemingway: Gauge of Morale," in *Ernest Hemingway: The Man and His Work*, John K. M. McCaffery, ed., p. 252. Essay originally published in *The Wound and the Bow* (New York: Oxford University Press, 1947).

ingway had learned in Spain, an intimation of a Hemingway who had found the thwarted ideal clear and radiant again through the martyrdom of the Spanish masses."[9] Kazin goes on to relate the story, in spirit, to *For Whom the Bell Tolls*. Each view touches on only part of the story's worth. Wilson's comments ignore the details which give the story a specific location and a particular meaning, while Kazin's use of terms like "thwarted ideal" and "martyrdom of the Spanish people" implies an ideological interpretation which the story will not support.

Only in "Old Man at the Bridge," of all his writings about Spain, was Hemingway able to objectify his view of the war without violating in any way his own artistic sensibility, for only in this story does he avoid the temptation to moralize his song. Ray B. West has pointed out that the tendency toward explicit moralizing is a consistent failing in Hemingway's work,[10] and it is one which does serious damage, as we have seen, to *The Fifth Column* and *For Whom the Bell Tolls*. In this story, however, there is no preaching, no attempt to use clichés or rhetoric to enforce the meaning. The meaning is nevertheless clear, and it is the same meaning which Hemingway tried to communicate directly in *The Fifth Column* when he had Max say, "You do it so men will not have to fear ill health or old age. . . ."[11] This statement might be the text for "Old Man at the Bridge," but because the text is only implied, the moral does not obtrude.

One other poet, Charles Donnelly, deserves consideration here. An Irishman who was a member of the International Brigades, Donnelly was killed in February, 1937, at the age

[9] Alfred Kazin, *On Native Grounds* (Garden City: Doubleday & Co., 1956), pp. 262–63.
[10] Ray B. West, "Ernest Hemingway: The Failure of Sensibility," in William Van O'Connor, ed., *Forms of Modern Fiction*, p. 94.
[11] *The Fifth Column*, p. 79.

of twenty-six. It was apparently the practice of soldiers in the Brigades to paste their writings to *periódicos murales* or, more prosaically, bulletin boards. The first publication of Donnelly's two poems was on such a mural, the poems having been found among the papers he left when he was killed. They were worth saving.

Donnelly's poems, like a great deal of modern verse, show the influence of Hopkins in their deliberate use of harsh sound patterns and gnarled syntax. "The Tolerance of Crows," which Spender and Lehmann chose for inclusion in *Poems for Spain*, is spare to the point of starkness:

> Death comes in quantity from solved
> Problems on maps, well-ordered dispositions,
> Angles of elevation and direction;
>
> Comes innocent from tools children might
> Love, retaining under pillows,
> Innocently impales on any flesh.
>
> And with flesh falls apart the mind
> That trails thought from the mind that cuts
> Thought clearly for a waiting purpose.
>
> Progress of poison in the nerves and
> Discipline's collapse's halted.
> Body awaits the tolerance of crows.[12]

The fact of death is the more powerfully conveyed here because of the apparent detachment of the writer and his description of the causes of death: "solved problems on maps, well-ordered dispositions." The agents of death are themselves

---

[12] Charles Donnelly, in Stephen Spender and John Lehmann, eds., *Poems for Spain*, pp. 50–51. The poem is also printed in Edwin Rolfe's *The Lincoln Battalion* (New York: Veterans of the Abraham Lincoln Brigade, 1939), pp. 73–74, where line 11 appears as "Discipline's collapse is halted."

innocent; they might even have been toys in a happier dispensation. Death itself comes after the wounding has led to the collapse of discipline. The poem is very close to the central impulses of twentieth-century literature toward simplicity and toward the use of images (rather than emotionally weighted description) as the source of emotion. The language is carefully neutral, and the more ironic for being so.

Irony is the dominant mode of Donnelly's other poem, but in this somewhat longer work the subject is not death but the fate of the hero.[13] John Cornford had dealt with a similar subject in "Full Moon at Tierz," which speculates upon the need of the frightened private man to appear publicly brave lest he weaken the cause for which he fights. Donnelly is more concerned with what happens to the man once his heroic deeds are past, when he is not weighted down with political responsibility. Public figures will always exploit the private deeds of others for their own selfish purposes, Donnelly says, and paradoxically, the more unselfish and idealistic the deeds are, the more easily they can be exploited and so corrupted:

> Between rebellion as a private study and the public
> Defiance is simple action which will flicker
> Catlike, for spring. Whether at nerve-roots is secret
> Iron, there's no diviner can tell, only the moment can show.
> Simple and unclear moment, on a morning utterly different
> And under circumstances different from what you'd expected.
>
> Your flag is public over granite. Gulls fly above it.
> Whatever the issue of the battle is, your memory
> Is public, for them to pull awry with crooked hands,
> Moist eyes. And the villages' reputation will be built on
> Inaccurate accounts of your campaigns. You're name for orators,
> Figure stone-struck beneath damp Dublin sky.

[13] Charles Donnelly, "Poem," in Alvah Bessie, ed., *The Heart of Spain*, pp. 162–63.

In a delaying action, perhaps, on a hillside in remote parish,
Outposts correctly placed, retreat secured to wood, bridge mined
Against pursuit, sniper may sight you carelessly contoured.
Or death may follow years in strait confinement, where diet
Is uniform as ceremony, lacking only fruit
Or on the barracks square before the sun casts shadow.

Name, subject of all considered words, praise and blame
Irrelevant, the public talk which sounds the same on hollow
Tongue as true, you'll be with Parnell and with Pearse.
Name alderman will raise a cheer with, teacher make reference
Oblique in class, and boys and women spin gum of sentiment
On qualities attributed in error.

Man, dweller in mountain huts, possessor of colored mice,
Skillful in minor manual turns, patron of obscure subjects, of
Gaelic swordsmanship and medieval armory,
The technique of the public man, the masked servilities are
Not for you, Master of military trade, you give
Like Raleigh, Lawrence, Childers, your service but not yourself.

The ostensible subject of "Poem" is not, of course, the war
in Spain. Donnelly's allusions are primarily to heroes of
England or the Irish rebellions, and the poem utilizes what
must have been the poet's childhood experience of hero-
worship. The Irish experience, however, is clearly informed
and directed by what Donnelly must have learned of heroism
and bravery in the Spanish War. The poem shows, in any case,
a skillful hand with irony, sometimes based on literary ante-
cedents, as the final stanza, for example, recalls the Sophoclean
chorus from *Antigone*. That Donnelly was not an experienced
poet is demonstrated by the ending of the first stanza, where
the concrete imagery associated with physical courage is unfortunately blunted by the prosaic "on a morning utterly different / And under circumstances different from what you'd

expected." But the lapse is only momentary, and Donnelly returns immediately to the specific image of the flag, "public over granite." The third stanza holds a special interest because of the similarity between one of the incidents its describes and the central situation of Hemingway's *For Whom the Bell Tolls*. Donnelly, though technically a "modern" poet in the relative freedom of his verse (variant rhythm, absence of rhyme, erratic line length) and his attempt to gain conciseness by omitting the articles, has constructed "Poem" carefully, each stanza adding to what has gone before and preparing for the climax of the final stanza, with its amused rather than bitter commentary on man, and its sympathy for heroes.

It is worth noting that Donnelly makes a number of observations in "Poem" which are rare in the literature of the Spanish Civil War. Unlike those (Cornford is the obvious example) who are so dedicated to the cause that they think only of what their deeds may contribute to it, Donnelly recognizes that the public acclaim for deeds of valor will inevitably distort the nature of the deeds. He makes it clear, and all the evidence strongly suggests that he is correct in this, that heroism is very nearly an accident, and that its occurrence is unpredictable; it is not conferred upon a man by his beliefs or by the organizations to which he belongs. The war in Spain, is, in this respect at least, like other wars. Finally, there is nothing in the poem to suggest that this realistic appraisal ought to make the volunteer regret his commitment nor the intelligent soldier give up thinking. Donnelly's attitude is wry and more than a little sad, but the implication of the poem is that he will go on fighting without trying to deny what he knows.

Apart from these few brief works, only one book rises to the level of art, and that is the generally acknowledged classic of the Spanish Civil War, George Orwell's *Homage to Cata-*

lonia.[14] For almost fifteen years after its original English publication in 1938, the book was almost entirely ignored. The
original edition sold very badly, and no American publication was attempted until 1952. Since then, this memoir has
begun to receive the attention it deserves, although it has received less sympathetic criticism than have Orwell's novels.

The reasons for the long neglect of the book and for its
more recent resurrection from the dusty shelves of libraries
are closely related to the very different political situations of
the late thirties on the one hand and the fifties and sixties on
the other. Orwell's book was certain to be met by indifference
when it was first published. Among other things, *Homage* argued that the Communists were playing a dirty game in Spain,
that there was a good deal of unsavory intrigue among de-
clared allies on the Loyalist side, and that the press of Great
Britain and the United States failed to report the war with
even a little accuracy. On the other hand, Orwell also made
it clear that he hoped the Loyalists would win, that the Roman
Catholic Church in Spain was an oppressive and vicious organization, and that Franco was a disaster. Since most of the
British reading public, like the intelligentsia, was committed
to one side or the other, and to the belief that their side was
not only right but near-perfect, the book could hardly expect
a sympathetic audience. But the same book, in the atmosphere of the fifties, was able to provide reassurance to those
who needed it that the Communists were devils, 'way back then.

Homage was written and published in 1938, after Orwell
had returned to England but before the war had ended. Unlike
most of the other personal memoirs of the war in Spain (*Men
in Battle* is another exception), *Homage* was not intended as
propaganda for the Loyalist cause. Orwell knew that his book,

[14] Boston: Beacon Press, 1952. References here (page references incorporated in the text) are to the 1955 edition.

or any other, was not likely to help that cause very much. The aim of the book was to clear up what Orwell thought were two major misconceptions: the myths about the life of the soldier in Spain, which had been created by books like *Volunteer in Spain*, and the myths about the nature of the struggle, which had been carefully nurtured by most of the left-wing press. If other books also claimed to tell the truth about Spain, Orwell's is unusual in being based upon what he had seen and experienced, and in the author's warning that the nature of truth is not always clear, nor his story the only story:

I believe that on an issue such as this no one is or can be completely truthful. It is difficult to be certain about anything except what you have seen with your own eyes, and consciously or unconsciously everyone writes as a partisan . . . Beware of my partisanship, my mistakes of fact and the distortion inevitably caused by my having seen only one corner of events. (pp. 230–31)

Orwell's Spanish experience is largely the story of a series of accidents which placed him in particular places at critical times, and it is at first glance a simple story. He arrived in Barcelona in December of 1936, ostensibly as a correspondent, but he very soon joined the militia, because "at that time and in that atmosphere it seemed the only conceivable thing to do." (p. 23) At this juncture most of the armed men on the Loyalist side, especially in Catalonia, were in the militia units of labor unions and left-wing political parties. Because of the papers he carried, Orwell was enrolled in the militia of the small, independent left-wing party, POUM, and after the usual minimum of useless training was shipped to the front in Aragon, near Zaragoza. The front was inactive at the time, and he was quickly made aware of the vital concerns of trench warfare in Spain: "firewood, food, tobacco, candles and the enemy. In winter on the Zaragoza front they were important in that order, with the enemy a bad last." (p. 23)

Transferred to another sector of the same front, near Huesca, Orwell finally took part in a battle, an action typical in its indecisiveness of most battles in most wars. (pp. 86–100) He was on leave from this front and in Barcelona when the fighting broke out there over the government's move to incorporate the militia units into the Popular Army and to appropriate the arms still held by the labor unions and political parties; the heart of *Homage* is the description of this fighting. When it had ended, Orwell returned to the front, was wounded by a bullet in the neck, and ultimately was invalided back to Barcelona. There, as a member of an outlawed militia, he found himself in danger of imminent arrest and possible execution, and with his wife he fled to France.

Orwell's attempt to provide an accurate account of the May fighting in Barcelona, and to examine the reasons behind that weird interlude, is the most important part of *Homage*, but since the book is arranged in a chronological pattern he deals first with his experiences as a soldier. His aim in the first part of the book is like that of Alvah Bessie in *Men in Battle*. Both show that even in Spain sleeping in the mud, struggling to keep warm, and firing and being fired at in anger were experiences less pleasurable and more dangerous than attending protest meetings or going on Young Communist League hikes. But the similarity ends here, for Orwell describes events in the trenches to prepare the reader for more important later events, while Bessie's events seem almost to exist in a void. More important, Orwell is the better writer, with the ability to select from his experiences the critical incident or the typical gesture and to use it to illuminate his picture of war.

Orwell never permits his material to force him to the plodding, repetitious catalogues of events which make *Men in Battle*, for all its sincerity, ultimately a tiresome book. Orwell's sense of the ridiculous is most useful in his observations on the soldier's life:

All of us were lousy by this time; though still cold it was warm enough for that. I have had a big experience of body vermin of various kinds, and for sheer beastliness the louse beats everything I have encountered. Other insects, mosquitoes for instance, make you suffer more, but at least they aren't *resident* vermin. The human louse resembles a tiny lobster, and he lives chiefly in your trousers. Short of burning all your clothes there is no known way of getting rid of him. Down the seams of your trousers he lays his glittering white eggs, like tiny grains of rice, which hatch out and breed families of their own at horrible speed. I think the pacifists might find it helpful to illustrate their pamphlets with enlarged photographs of lice. Glory of war, indeed! In war *all* soldiers are lousy, at least when it is warm enough. The men who fought at Verdun, at Waterloo, at Flodden, at Senlac, at Thermopylae — every one of them had lice crawling over his testicles. (p. 76)

Passages like this show Orwell at his best — realistic as anyone could wish, but with his characteristic touch of outraged irony which debunks all grandiose notions of heroism, whether in this war or in any other. Only a very few writers, Orwell, Charles Donnelly, and perhaps Humphrey Slater, saw that the war in Spain was not altogether unique, was not the glorious crusade which the party-line organs (and liberal and left-wing journals in general) pretended it was. For the men who did the actual fighting, it was a war like any other, lice and all.

Orwell has other methods of deflating notions of exaggerated heroism. One of the most effective is employed in his description of his first departure for the front, which focuses on the personal discomfort and the reactions of the individual soldier, in sharp contrast to the description of a similar scene by John Sommerfield:

I remember vividly the torchlit scene — the uproar and excitement, the red flags flapping in the torchlight, the massed ranks of militiamen with their knapsacks on their backs and their rolled blankets worn bandolier-like across the shoulder; and the shouting and the clatter of boots and tin pannikins, and then a tremendous and finally successful hissing for silence; and then some political commissar standing beneath a huge rolling red banner and making us a speech in Catalan. Finally they marched us to the station, taking the longest route, three or four miles, so as to show us to the whole town. In the Ramblas they halted us while a borrowed band played some revolutionary tune or other. Once again the conquering hero stuff — shouting and enthusiasm, red flags and red and black flags everywhere, friendly crowds thronging the pavement to have a look at us, women waving wildly from the windows. How natural it all seemed then; how remote and impossible now! The train was packed so tight with men that there was barely room even on the floor, let alone on the seats. At the last moment Williams' wife came running down the platform and gave us a bottle of wine and a foot of that bright red sausage which tastes of soap and gives you diarrhoea. (pp. 13–14)

The method here might be called the double-delayed anticlimax; whenever Orwell shows us a side of war which might make us think that it is glamorous and exciting, he walks us three or four miles and produces the laxative sausage tasting of soap to remind us that modern war is never a boy's game.

That such reminders are necessary is explained in Orwell's essay "Looking Back on the Spanish War," published a few years after *Homage*. Recalling the "romantic war-mongering muck" used in British and American left-wing papers to describe the war, he points out that the very people who had exploited the horrors of war for political purposes during the early thirties conveniently forgot about them when the political winds shifted and violence again became acceptable. But the facts did not change:

The essential horror of army life . . . is barely affected by the nature of the war you happen to be fighting in. Discipline, for instance, is ultimately the same in all armies. . . . The picture of war set forth in books like *All Quiet on the Western Front* is substantially true.

Bullets hurt, corpses stink, men under fire are often so frightened that they wet their trousers. It is true that the social background from which an army springs will colour its training, tactics, and general efficiency, and also that being in the right can bolster up morale, though this affects the civilian population more than the troops. . . . But the laws of nature are not suspended for a "red" army any more than for a "white" one. A louse is a louse and a bomb is a bomb, even though the cause you are fighting for happens to be just.[15]

Orwell's portrayal of the soldier's experience is as crisp and as moving as anything to have come out of the Spanish Civil War, or for that matter any other war, but as I have said, in *Homage* this picture is primarily used as a means of preparing the reader to understand the context of the later events. Orwell's discussion of the war in *Homage* illustrates his later statement that "The outcome of the Spanish war was settled in London, Paris, Rome, Berlin — at any rate, not in Spain."[16] It is a truism that nothing that happened in Spain during the war had as much effect on its outcome as the diplomatic actions of the great powers. It is also true, however, that among the events in Spain itself, those which took place behind the front lines were probably more important than any of the battles, and that one of the most crucial of these events was the May fighting in Barcelona in 1937. This fighting is the climax of Orwell's book.

The confused and confusing political situation on the Loyalist side has been the subject of a number of studies, and cannot be fully explained here.[17] But some understanding of the Barcelona fighting and of the special situation in Catalonia

[15] "Looking Back on the Spanish War," in *Such, Such Were the Joys* (New York: Harcourt, Brace, 1952), p. 130. Essay originally dated 1943.
[16] *Ibid.*, p. 146.
[17] Fuller discussions are available in Salvador de Madariága, *Spain: A Modern History* (New York: Frederick Praeger, 1958); Brenan, *The Spanish Labyrinth*; and Thomas, *The Spanish Civil War*. The latter is the most complete and probably the most accurate.

are essential to an understanding of Orwell's book, and I shall try to sketch them briefly.

By the spring of 1937 the Loyalist central government was dominated by the left-wing of the Socialist party, a group which was tied to the Third International and to the Spanish Communist party; the latter had gained a measure of strength wholly disproportionate to its pre-Civil War size because it functioned as the regent of the Soviet Union, but the Spanish Communist party remained too small numerically to take control in its own name. Neither Socialist nor Communist party was strong in Catalonia, but they had managed to combine various Socialist groups into the PSUC (*Partit Socialista Unificat de Catalunya*), and they relied upon this group as their agent in Catalonia. The PSUC, however, had to depend for stability upon the Anarchists, who derived their inspiration from Bakunin rather than from Marx, and whose notorious instability and continuing distrust of all governments made the Catalonian situation highly volatile. Adding to the confusion was the long Catalan tradition of agitation for regional autonomy, essentially a middle-class movement unrelated to the anarchism of the working class. This movement had finally been successful in the early days of the Spanish Republic.[18]

There were, therefore, three main groups struggling for power in Catalonia: the PSUC, allied to the central government; the Catalonian *Generalitat*, established before the war and representative of the bourgeoisie; and the *ad hoc* Committee of Fifteen, established in the early days of the fighting to direct left-wing opposition to the Insurgent revolt because it was feared that the Generalitat would be insufficiently militant — the Committee of Fifteen was dominated by the FAI (*Federación Anarchista Ibérica*). The Committee continued

[18] Madariaga, *Spain: A Modern History*, pp. 400–03.

to direct military operations in the northeast, to the considerable annoyance of the central government in Madrid. Early in 1937, the Madrid regime undertook to establish a unified command which would incorporate the militia units formerly under party or union orders, a move which received scant support from the Committee of Fifteen. The PSUC, acting for the central government, was reluctant to move directly against the FAI or the Committee, which had too much popular support to be easy victims, but it could and did put pressure on the POUM. The POUM was a natural target, for although in practice it was allied with the FAI, it was a small and relatively powerless group. Suppressing it and appropriating the arms of its militia would show the power of the government. Because it was a Marxist group, but independent of Moscow, the POUM could be, and was, labeled "Trotskyist," a term roughly synonymous with Fascist and traitorous in the vocabulary of the time, but carrying the additional stigma of apostasy from the true faith. It was charged that this group had been negotiating with the Insurgents, and that its militiamen were therefore likely to turn their guns on their erstwhile allies whenever these negotiations proved fruitful. The charge was patently absurd, and has never been taken seriously by objective historians.

In Barcelona, however, the charges seemed extremely serious, and much of the bitterness of Orwell's story of the Barcelona fighting is accounted for by the attempt to label the POUM as a treasonous organization. But for these charges, Orwell says, he would have been willing to accept the official explanation of the causes of the incident. As it is, Orwell's analysis gains credibility from the fact that in the beginning he had been uninterested in the political differences on the Loyalist side, and had joined the POUM militia by accident. (p. 47) He had been generally unsympathetic to the POUM viewpoint, and as a soldier at the front "preferred the Communist viewpoint to that of the P.O.U.M." (p. 62) After his front-line hitch with the POUM, he decided to join the Communist-dominated International Column, and had taken steps toward that end at the beginning of his leave in Barcelona (p. 117), but before definite arrangements could be made the fighting had begun. By the time it was over, four days later, the anti-POUM propaganda was accusing all the men in its militia of the gravest crimes:

This, then, was what they were saying about us: we were Trotskyists, Fascists, traitors, murderers, cowards, spies and so forth. I admit it was not pleasant, especially when one thought of some of the people who were responsible for it. It is not a nice thing to see a Spanish boy of fifteen carried down the line on a stretcher, with a dazed white face looking out from among the blankets, and to think of the sleek persons in London and Paris who are writing pamphlets to prove that this boy is a Fascist in disguise. (pp. 64–65)

This was bad enough, but in essence it was the usual interparty bickering on the left given added seriousness because men were killing each other. But the political quarrels were in this case little more than symptoms of what was to Orwell the real stake in the fighting: the revolution, and the attempt to betray it. For the early days of the war had been a time of genuine revolution in many parts of Spain, in which industries had been collectivized and large estates expropriated and divided among the peasants. In early 1937 the revolution had been halted and even pushed back, as the government undertook a policy whose aim was to show that Republican Spain was just another bourgeois democracy where foreign investments would be perfectly safe. Most of the other memoirs of Spain, and contemporary analyses of the Civil

War, paid little attention to the revolution.[19] Many of the foreign volunteers were unaware of it, and a good many volunteers as well as correspondents and observers accepted a party line which denied its reality. For Orwell, whose approach was nondoctrinaire and whose chief interest was in the fact that somewhere in the world the lower classes had briefly attained power, the revolution was of first importance.

It was the revolutionary atmosphere of Barcelona, late in 1936, that inspired Orwell to join the fighting in the first place, and that sustained him until he returned to the city at the end of April, 1937, to find the revolutionary atmosphere gone. The account of his return to the city reveals as well as any passage in the book Orwell's hopes for the Spanish people, and the dashing of those hopes:

In the train, all the way to Barcelona, the atmosphere of the front persisted; the dirt, the noise, the discomfort, the ragged clothes, the feeling of privation, comradeship and equality. The train, already full of militiamen when it left Barbastro, was invaded by more and more peasants at every station on the line; peasants with bundles of vegetables, with terrified fowls which they carried head-downwards, with sacks which looped and writhed all over the floor and were discovered to be full of live rabbits — finally with a quite considerable flock of sheep which were driven into the compartments and wedged into every empty space. The militiamen shouted revolutionary songs which drowned the rattle of the train and kissed their hands or waved red and black handkerchiefs to every pretty girl along the line. Bottles of wine and of anis, the filthy Aragonese liqueur, travelled from hand to hand. With the Spanish goat-skin water-bottles you can squirt a jet of wine right across a railway carriage into your friend's mouth, which saves a lot of trouble. Next to me a black-eyed boy of fifteen was recounting sensational and, I do not doubt, completely untrue stories of his own exploits at the front to two old leather-faced peasants

[19] An exception is Franz Borkenau, *The Spanish Cockpit* (London: Faber & Faber, 1937).

who listened open-mouthed. Presently the peasants undid their bundles and gave us some sticky dark-red wine. Everyone was profoundly happy, more happy than I can convey. But when the train had rolled through Sabadell and into Barcelona, we stepped into an atmosphere that was scarcely less alien to us and our kind than if this had been Paris or London. (pp. 108–09)

The arrival in Barcelona was a distinct letdown for Orwell, but worse was to follow. The chapter dealing with the prelude to the actual fighting and with the outbreak (pp. 121–49) is a story of mounting tension, suspicion, and hatred among people supposedly on the same side. The trouble lasted for only a few days (May 3–7) and even at its height there were occasions when the fighters on opposing sides talked with each other cordially, but the fighting was real enough. Within a day or two the entire city began to run short of food, and the pressures for a settlement soon became irresistible. The POUM, short of arms and ammunition and ignored by its Anarchist allies, capitulated. The whole episode was, for Orwell, profoundly disillusioning.

At this stage, Orwell inserts a chapter explaining the political situation, a device to which he has recourse several times in *Homage*. In beginning these chapters, he warns the reader to skip if he is interested in the narrative but not in the political involutions of his experience. Some readers have taken him seriously, and there have been occasional objections that these chapters do break up the continuity of the narrative. To so object is not only to reveal considerable naïveté, but also to underestimate Orwell's capacity for irony. For if the action of *Homage* has a theme, it is that the fighting and the other events can be understood only in terms of the politics which motivated the events, and that to anyone who does not understand the politics, the fighting must appear to be sheer madness.

These political chapters, although their insertion is perhaps slightly awkward, are therefore essential to the book, and on the whole probably the best method Orwell could have used for conveying the necessary information about the underlying motives for action. Certainly his method is preferable to the only real alternative: including political analysis as part of the description of the action, which would have been much more obtrusive and much more annoying. The political chapters perform another function for the reader, because they convey three fundamental elements of Orwell's character: his belief that the truth about events in war or politics is knowable, his belief that such knowledge is of first importance (in *1984* one of the abuses that he regards as most frightening is the ability of the regime to change the past by rewriting history), and his understanding that such truth is never simple. These are distinctive elements in all of Orwell's work, the novels and the essays as well as *Homage*, and they are worth bringing up again because Orwell's critics have tended to ignore the last of the three.

It is true enough that in one way Orwell was a simple man. He was not given to abstract thought, and one of his sympathetic critics has written that "Orwell was not prolific of ideas; he had a few basic ones, which he repeated over and over." [20] But a number of writers have gone beyond this insight to the oversimplification that a kind of simple decency was the essential element of Orwell's character and of his writings:

The common element in all George Orwell's writing was a sense of decency. [21]

. . . As if he could not resist making at least one remark about Orwell himself, he said suddenly in a very simple and matter-of-fact

[20] John Wain, "Orwell in Perspective," *New World Writing* 12 (New York: New American Library of World Literature, 1957), pp. 84–85.

[21] John Atkins, *George Orwell* (London: John Calder, 1954), p. 1.

way, "He was a virtuous man." And we sat there, agreeing at length about this statement, finding a curious pleasure in talking about it.[22]

Orwell spoke with the simple honesty of a man about to die.[23]

There is, as Lionel Trilling has pointed out, something old-fashioned about the terms customarily used to describe Orwell — decency, virtue, simple honesty. They seem to place him in some earlier time, when politics was neither so complicated nor so desperate a matter as it has come to be in the twentieth century; and when "one's simple, direct, undeceived intelligence"[24] was sufficient to an understanding of the problems of the day. But the use of such terms reveals more about the critics who use them than about Orwell.

Orwell may have shared with these critics a nostalgia for a simpler past — his yearning for a simple world in which men who shared goals could work together toward those goals is implicit in everything he wrote, and his idealization of an ordered past is manifest in *Coming Up for Air* — but he did not permit it to lead him to the conclusion that the present is also simple if one will only accept one of the dogmas that says it is simple. Orwell knew his experience to be a uniquely modern one, and his reaction to it was untypical only in that he was far less prone than most of his contemporaries to devote a good deal of time and energy to embracing dogmas and then reacting against them. Orwell knew as well as any of his contemporaries that all fighting faiths are less than perfect, that all utopias are illusions. But where others abandoned the faith and the fighting or denied the illusions, Orwell accepted what he saw and still maintained that it was not only possible

[22] Lionel Trilling, Introduction to 1955 edition of *Homage to Catalonia*, p. viii.
[23] John Dos Passos, *The Theme Is Freedom* (New York: Dodd, Mead, 1956), p. 146.
[24] Trilling, p. x.

but necessary to make choices in the light of continually changing realities, and to defend those choices. If the Loyalist cause was less than holy, if the revolution had been betrayed, if he himself had very nearly given his life for that cause only to be branded a traitor and forced to flee the country — that was too bad, and must be made known, but Orwell could not react to it by crying down a plague on all houses and retreating to the study of the classics, or of one's own navel.

History is conflict, and when history is being made it is important to see that neither side is perfect or near perfection, and equally important to make a choice: "I hope they win their war and drive all foreigners out of Spain, Germans, Russians, and Italians alike. This war, in which I played so ineffectual a part, has left me with memories that are mostly evil, and yet I do not wish that I had missed it." (p. 230)

Such a response may appear simple in its results, but it is not based upon a simplistic view of the world. As a modern man, Orwell was aware of the complexities of his world, and though he might deplore them he was fully involved in them. This is evident in the political chapters of *Homage*, as it is in most of his writings. His analysis of the political situation in Spain is lucid but not oversimplified: it was wrong of the government to suppress the revolution and to outlaw the POUM; at the same time there was a case to be made for a unified government and a centrally directed army, and neither of these was possible if the revolution went forward and the POUM retained control of an independent militia. Still, the Barcelona fighting was part of an attempt at Communist control of Loyalist Spain, and this was bad; on the other hand, the Communists did offer discipline and a program for winning the war. The choices are not "simple." A "simple" man would probably never have seen the choices as Orwell saw them, certainly not with the same clarity combined with an awareness of complexity. It is perhaps one of his major virtues that Orwell tried never to evade an issue or a choice, even while he forbade himself the luxury of self-deception in describing the situations in which choices had to be made.

After all, though, a man would have to be a saint to avoid self-deception entirely, and Orwell was no saint, proto-Christian though Christopher Hollis tried to make him. Orwell had a faith, and in any faith there is a measure of self-deception. Orwell's faith was in the democratic tendencies of an England that had preserved virtues worth having and in the power of those virtues to help in evolving a society more nearly classless and just than any which had yet existed. He had faith also that the working class "in the long run . . . remains the most reliable enemy of fascism." [25] The flaw in this faith was his acknowledgment that the articles of his faith were imperfect; his country had, after all, produced an aristocracy whose chief distinctions were "stupidity, unconscious sabotage, an infallible instinct for doing the wrong thing." [26] His belief in the ultimate reliability of the working class is symbolized by the Italian militiaman he met in Barcelona who made a deep impression on Orwell, [27] but the militiaman is not represented as any more typical of his class than the "little brute" at the front who threw a hand grenade into a campfire as a joke. (p. 26)

Toward the end of his life, having survived another and more destructive war, having seen that modern societies tend toward regimentation whether their official ideology be Fascist, Socialist, Democratic, or Communist, Orwell was overwhelmed

[25] "England, Your England," in *Such, Such Were the Joys*, pp. 200 ff. See also "Looking Back on the Spanish War," p. 144.

[26] "England, Your England," p. 222.

[27] See *Homage to Catalonia*, pp. 3–4, and "Looking Back on the Spanish War," pp. 149–53. The latter contains one of Orwell's few poems, which comes as close as Orwell ever did to sentimentality.

with a vision of the future that would come if his faith had been mistaken, if the democratic virtues could not prevent the abuses of freedom, if the antipathy of the working class to fascism only showed up in the very long run. But even that vision and its manifestation, the novel *1984*, are a part of Orwell's lifelong commitment to the critical examination of the world he lived in, and to the need to act on that examination. *1984* is in many ways a number of light years away from *Homage to Catalonia*, but they are on the same road.

7. Conclusion

THERE IS always the temptation, in dealing with literary phenomena, to exaggerate the importance of our special interests, and I have no wish to fall into this trap in discussing the literature of the Spanish Civil War. The political history of our time is complex and confused, and it remains for scholars and historians of the future to determine the ultimate significance of the events with which we have lived. The Spanish Civil War was one of those events, one among the many which have influenced the political attitudes of the Anglo-American intelligentsia. Disillusion with the Soviet Union and consequently with communism and the related decline of the left would in all likelihood have occurred even if the war in Spain had not taken its peculiar direction. The process had, after all, set in earlier in representatives of western European and American literary circles who had seen the future and learned to fear and mistrust it, whether it worked or not — Edmund Wilson and André Gide were only two among many to experience this disillusion. The Moscow Trials, at least in part because of the mock-trials in London which found the defendants innocent, had revealed a side of the Soviet experiment deeply troubling to many who had been sympathetic, while the Nazi-Soviet Treaty of 1939, Russia's subsequent part in the dismemberment of Poland, and the Winter War with Finland played their roles in the drama of disillusion.

The effects of disillusionment were felt more strongly in Great Britain and the United States than in such continental countries as France and Italy. In the years since World War II, it has become increasingly unfashionable in the English-speaking world to display admiration for, or even interest in, the legacy of Karl Marx. No British or American literary figure of the stature of Sartre or Silone has evinced any enthusiasm for communism, even as an abstraction. Some of the reasons for this divided response are purely historical. The left-wing movement generally, and the Communist party specifically, never had the kind of working-class appeal in the United States and Great Britain which gave the French Communist party a broad popular base even during the thirties, and which has enabled both the French and the Italian parties to poll impressive votes in every election held in those countries since the end of World War II. Furthermore, the Communists in those countries were prominent in the partisan resistance movements, and the Communist parties attained a degree of popular approval because of their underground role during World War II. British and American intellectuals, on the other hand, began to draw away from communism when they began to see its darker side, and when they realized that Marxism had failed to interest the agricultural and industrial workers in their countries. At that, the much-maligned intellectuals probably saw the nature of international communism before the politicians did.

The question of why Americans and Britons reacted differently than did the French, the Italians, and others cannot, how-

ever, be answered simply by saying that resistance fighters
and mass-based political movements gave some national Communist parties more prestige than others. Even a qualified
answer to the question is more complex and more obscure,
and it requires some broad (and therefore tentative) generalizations about national experience, as well as a more precise
analysis of the effects of the Spanish Civil War.

The key generalization here is that politics has been, for
the last hundred years at least, less ideological in its American
and British manifestations than in their continental counterparts. A necessary further distinction is that the British have
been, naturally enough, closer to the continental European
experience in this than have the Americans, but in spite of
this I believe that the generalization holds. Not the least important of the distinctions of the late President Kennedy was
his pragmatic grasp of the fact that American politics, both
domestic and international, has always been essentially pragmatic. By way of contrast, an almost hysterical insistence on
the moral basis of American foreign policy has from time to
time handicapped United States handling of foreign affairs.
For a brief time in the thirties, it is true, American politics
and American culture took on an ideological tinge, but this
was not in any genuine sense a revival of an American tradition, Calverton and Geismar to the contrary. The customary
response of the American intellectual to politics has been indifference or, in the rare cases of men like Henry Adams, disgust. When an American writer attempts to promote an ideology he is likely to be surprised by the results: Upton Sinclair
may have wanted a Socialist America when he wrote *The
Jungle*; what he got was a Pure Food and Drug Act, a pragmatic answer to a practical problem.

The British case is not dissimilar, except superficially. The
class basis of the English party system may have seemed to

Marx to confirm his theories, and even today that system is more rooted in economic rivalries than is the American party system, but British intellectuals have been no more politically oriented, over the years, than their American counterparts. Again, the rare exceptions tend to prove the generalization: Shaw's political ideas were often naïve, sometimes to the point of silliness. Once more, the thirties seemed to have changed things, but the change was hardly deep-seated, and it passed sooner than anyone would have guessed when it began. Because the British are more likely than the Americans to tolerate eccentricity in their great men, we sometimes have the feeling that British intellectuals remain more ideologically oriented than their American equivalents, but it remains true that Bloomsbury is closer to the heart of British intellectualism than is the London School of Economics.

The literature of the two decades since the end of World War II provides a great deal of evidence for these generalizations, and it is worth examining certain aspects of this literature in some detail in order to see more clearly the changes in our literary attitudes. One obvious example of these changes is the postwar American novel. It is true that the young men who came back from the war in 1945–46 were for the most part products of the thirties, and the first wave of war novels showed that they were still under the influence of prewar ideologies. Novels like *The Naked and the Dead, The Young Lions, The End of My Life,* and *The Conquerors* all are politically oriented, in greater or less degree. But these were the first postwar novels of their authors, all of whom would later come to ignore political theory as a meaningful source of understanding. Significantly, all of these novels were written between 1945 and 1950. The second wave of war novels (for example Anton Myrer's *The Big War,* Glenn Sire's *The Deathmakers,* and James Jones's *From Here to Eternity* and *The*

Thin Red Line) reflects almost no interest in politics whatever. The reaction against political ideology did not set in all
at once, but its force was irresistible.

It is also important that the fiction of World War II was not
a literature of disillusion to the extent that the novels of the
first Great War had been. The later novels reveal horror and
disgust; their authors would be less than human if they did
not. But the element of surprise is lacking, along with the sense
of betrayal. In *A Farewell to Arms*, Hemingway expressed the
outrage of a generation which had fought a war for high-
sounding slogans and found the slogans meaningless; they
had been betrayed by their leaders and had, in one way or
another, made their separate peace. The same sense of betrayal does not appear in the literature of World War II,
because the men who wrote about that war knew what to expect,
and their betrayals had come earlier. In part, of course, their
attitude shows that they had read Hemingway and Remarque
and the disillusioned writers of the twenties. But it seems to
me that they had also experienced their own disillusion, directly or vicariously, before the formal beginning of World
War II, in the Spanish Civil War. For the literature of that
war does contain the outraged sense of betrayal which we
find in Wilfred Owen and in Hemingway's early work; we
find in it, time after time, the echo of their implicit complaint:
"This is not the way we were told it would be; this war was
supposed to be different."

In a sense, the right of the novelists of World War II to
make this protest had been pre-empted by those who wrote
about Spain. Not in any simple sense, since there was not a
great deal of fictional expression of this emotion, but in the
sense that members of their generation had already expressed
for Mailer, Bourjaily, Vidal, and others the immediate horror.

Through the writings of Spender, Payne, Hemingway in a somewhat equivocal way, Humphrey Slater after the lapse of a few years, and through their own sense of the tragedy of Spain, the younger writers went to war knowing that they had been deprived of the right to easy disillusion. They might still be outraged, but they knew in advance what they must expect to see and experience. The sense of having missed their generation's crucial war when they failed to go to Spain is suggested by characters in a number of these novels: Hearn in *The Naked and the Dead*, Roberts in Heggen's *Mister Roberts*, and Whitacre in Shaw's *The Young Lions* all give expression to this attitude. These characters show the importance of the Spanish War as a register of shock.

It is this phenomenon which accounts for the widespread attitude of resignation toward the war itself, an attitude which dominated even the semi-official American stance in carrying out the war: This was a dirty job, the war was not glamorous, but it had to be done, and the sooner the better. Of all the phenomena of World War II, only the atomic bomb, at the very end, seemed to occasion much intellectual shock. Bombing of civilian populations was certainly more extensive and more destructive in the general war than it had been in Spain, but if you once accepted the possibility of the bombings of women and children in Barcelona or Guernica, Coventry and Cologne could not show you anything new. And the capacity of "shocklessness" seems to have extended to the Nazi attempt to exterminate the Jews. To be sure, William Golding has spoken of this as the phenomenon which accounts for the grimness of postwar British literature, and surely the knowledge that a highly civilized nation could undertake so horrible an enterprise has increased our awareness of man's potential for cruelty, but the recent controversy aroused by *The Deputy* seems to me to indicate that the annihilation of the Jews is still a fact which most of us have not really begun to believe. Certainly it has received very little attention in our literature.

But as I said before, the American and British understanding of politics has been less ideological in many ways than the continental attitude. In the literature of the Spanish Civil War itself, we have such examples as André Malraux's *L'espoir* to show us an understanding of the events in Spain entirely different from anything written in English. Malraux himself served the International Brigades and therefore, indirectly, the Communist party in Spain, but he did so without the illusions of an Ernest Hemingway or a Stephen Spender. I have been told, by an American critic who knew Malraux well, that as early as 1936 Malraux had spoken of the Moscow Trials in such a way as to indicate that he did not accept the official Soviet line on the trials and that he entertained no illusions about communism. But this did not prevent him from serving the party in Spain, with an attitude not unlike that which Sartre has taken in some of the postwar domestic controversies over communism in France. There is a kind of cynicism mixed with optimism not uncommon to Europeans which seems unavailable to British or Americans: Malraux could serve the party, and could write in *L'espoir* a novel at once disenchanted and hortatory, because like Sartre, like Silone, like Manes Sperber, he could at once see the imperfections of the Soviet Union and regard Marxism as the hope of the future. More than that, seeing the failings of the Soviet system and of the Communist parties it nurtured, he could still regard them as possible friends in the struggle for the end which he sought.

George Orwell is the only writer among those we have discussed who came close to sharing the attitudes of Malraux, but Orwell's vision of the world was influenced by a nationalism unknown among the continental intellectuals. Apart from Orwell, our own writers have followed the experience described by Edmund Wilson:

> . . . the conception of the dynamic Marxist will, the exaltation of the Marxist religion, seized the members of the professional classes like a capricious contagion or hurricane, which shakes one and leaves his neighbor standing, then returns to lay hold the second after the first has become quiet again. In the moment of seizure, each one of them saw a scroll unrolled from the heavens . . . (*Eight Essays*, 105–06)

The key word in this analysis is "hurricane." Once a cataclysm of this kind has passed, those who have survived it may remember it with awed respect or with loathing, they may speak of it with the affection of anguish reserved for the high points of a lifetime, they may hate the storm of their own responses to it, but they have no wish to see it come again. Most would prefer simply to forget that it had existed.

Among the writers, the true disillusionment came because many of them thought they had found in Marxism a means to contain and control the element of violence which is so clearly the center of twentieth-century life and of twentieth-century fiction. Whether or not literary naturalism is dead, its insight into the human predicament has continued to dominate our literature, for the simple enough reason that we have found that insight to be accurate. To writers born between 1900 and 1940, religion, nationalism, and democratic internationalism were unable to provide meaningful explanations of the upheavals of our time, or even means for comprehending them. This explains the desperation with which so many embraced Marxism in the thirties; it was the last chance, and for awhile it seemed the best chance. When the hurricane passed, those whom it had shaken came to believe that it had been no chance at all.

The literature of the Spanish Civil War and of the years

that have followed indicates how decisively we have abandoned the attempt to explore the relationship between politics
and violence, and this is a serious, possibly even fatal, blind
area not only in our literature but in our lives. Earlier times
were agitated by upheavals which were primarily religious,
economic, or social. In our own time the struggles which have
shaken the world, more violently than it has ever been shaken
before, have been fundamentally political. The ideologies
which have made the last fifty years the most revolutionary in
man's history have been political, but literature in English
has seemed almost entirely unaware that this is so, at least
during the last two decades. Our writers learned from the
Spanish Civil War that they had to be cautious and skeptical
in attempting to make use of the particular political dogmas,
but they have ignored the other lesson of that war, that politics
and violence are inextricably linked in our time.

This fact is less a condemnation of writers than an acknowledgment of the interdependence of literature and society. Our culture has turned away from political ideology ever
since the Spanish Civil War, the Soviet failings, and the dis-
integration of the Grand Alliance showed us that reality was
not so simple as simplistic ideologies made it seem. Economi-
cally, the members of the Western Alliance, including the
United States and Great Britain, have moved closer to a system which, for want of a better word, must be called socialism,
if we can think of that term without the pejorative meanings
attached to it by the strenuous efforts of those who hope to
reverse the development cycle followed by all of the great
industrial nations in this century. These nations have followed
this path, however, on pragmatic rather than ideological
grounds — another example of American cultural impact on
the rest of the world. Even Britain, which saw the success of
an ideologically oriented socialist movement, has seen that

movement become absorbed into the much-maligned "Establishment," and the practical results of the Socialist reform — health insurance, pensions, insurance of various kinds, governmental control of much of industry — have become part of the atmosphere which Amis, Osborne, Braine, and their contemporaries find so stifling. In the United States, increasing socialization is accompanied by ever more fervent vows of faith to "free enterprise," vows ironic even in the mouths of the most "conservative." The latter couple their cries for less "government interference" in business with demands for larger and larger "defense" budgets, for all the world as if the gigantic industries which dominate our economy did not depend precisely upon those defense budgets for a vital part of their income.

The lack of a credible ideology has of course been one of the West's handicaps in the Cold War. In the war for the allegiance of "uncommitted" nations, most of them former colonies, it is unlikely that we can sell capitalism, a system which in some countries depended entirely upon colonialism. We have ourselves moved a considerable distance from the classical concept of a capitalist economy, but we cannot admit even to ourselves that this is so, and our inability to make such an admission has effectively prevented us from creating an ideology based upon our experience and responsive to the demands of our position in the world. If, on the one hand, the writers and other intellectuals must bear a share of the responsibility for their failure to formulate such an ideology, a task which is logically theirs, a larger share of the responsibility must rest with the politicians and businessmen who have created a society terrified of facing its own contradictions and unwilling to understand them. It is difficult to blame the intelligentsia for looking outside their society to religion and myth for means of ordering at least their private visions.

For it is religion and mythological patterns which have appealed to writers as means of imparting order to experience, and therefore as means to artistic order. The situation which man has created has come to seem so appalling that man can no longer even attempt to comprehend it, nor live with the fact that he created it. The slaughter of the Jews, the mechanical destruction of World War II which we now know was only a primitive suggestion of the mechanical destruction we have now made possible, the existence of the most miserable and abject poverty and degradation in a world in which it would be a simple matter to end poverty and at least the cruder forms of misery, most of all the widespread conviction (so foreign to all of Western civilization) that men may no longer be able to control the monsters they have created — these facts of our existence have become so overwhelming that our writers have chosen one of two alternatives. Either they attempt, like Spender, to shore personal fragments against public ruins, hoping with fingers crossed that the chaos will not immediately destroy the private order; or they attempt to order the human experience in terms of a religious view which makes this world itself ephemeral, as Auden and his master Eliot have done. Our literature in the last twenty years suggests that this will be the pattern for the foreseeable future.

If this is the case, if we are in the middle of a literary era dominated by T. S. Eliot and Graham Greene at one end of the spectrum and by Stephen Spender and Lawrence Durrell at the other, the Spanish Civil War may well be increasingly neglected even as its importance for our literature becomes increasingly strong. For the literature with which this study has been concerned may well have been the final attempt in British and American literature to comprehend the violent nature of the modern world in terms of a political ideology.

Selected Bibliography

BOOKS

Aaron, Daniel. *Writers on the Left.* New York: Harcourt, Brace & World, 1961.

Anderson, Maxwell. *Key Largo.* New York: Harcourt, Brace, 1939.

Aney, Edith T. *British Poetry of Social Protest in the 1930's.* Unpublished Ph.D. dissertation, University of Pennsylvania, 1954.

Atkins, John. *George Orwell.* London: John Calder, 1954.

Baker, Carlos. *Hemingway: The Writer as Artist.* Princeton: Princeton University Press, 1952.

————, ed. *Hemingway and His Critics.* New York: Hill & Wang, 1961.

Barea, Arturo. *The Forging of a Rebel.* New York: Reynal & Hitchcock, 1946.

Barker, George. *Collected Poems: 1930–1955.* London: Faber & Faber, 1957.

Bates, Ralph. *The Olive Field.* New York: E. P. Dutton, 1936.

————. *Sirocco and Other Stories.* New York: Random House, 1939.

Benardete, M. J. and Rolfe Humphries, eds. . . . *And Spain Sings.* New York: Vanguard Press, 1937.

Bessie, Alvah, ed. *The Heart of Spain.* New York: Veterans of the Abraham Lincoln Brigade, 1952.

195

————. *Men in Battle.* New York: Charles Scribner's Sons, 1939 (edition used here, New York: Veterans of the Abraham Lincoln Brigade, 1954).

————. *The Un-Americans.* London: John Calder, 1957.

Blankfort, Michael. *The Brave and the Blind* (play). New York: Samuel French, 1937.

————. *The Brave and the Blind* (novel). Indianapolis: Bobbs-Merrill, 1940.

Borkenau, Franz. *The Spanish Cockpit.* London: Faber & Faber, 1937.

Bowers, Claude G. *My Mission to Spain.* New York: Simon & Schuster, 1954.

Brander, Lawrence. *George Orwell.* London: Longmans, Green & Co., 1954.

Brenan, Gerald. *The Face of Spain.* New York: Farrar, Straus & Cudahy, 1956.

————. *The Spanish Labyrinth.* New York: Macmillan Co., 1943.

Brennan, Frederick Hazlitt. *Memo to a Firing Squad.* New York: Alfred A. Knopf, 1943.

Brown, Alec. *Breakfast in Bed.* London: Boriswood, 1937.

Burden, Ruth. *Incident.* New York: Samuel French, 1937.

Burgum, Edwin Berry. *The Novel and the World's Dilemma.* New York: Oxford University Press, 1947.

Calmer, Alan, ed. *Salud!* New York: International Publishers, 1938.

Campbell, Roy. *Broken Record.* London: Boriswood, 1934.

————. *Collected Poems, 1957.* Chicago: Henry Regnery, 1957.

————. *Flowering Rifle.* New York, London: Longmans, Green & Co., 1939.

————. *Light on a Dark Horse.* Chicago: Henry Regnery, 1952.

Cattell, David T. *Communism and the Spanish Civil War.* Berkeley: University of California Press, 1955.

————. *Soviet Diplomacy in the Spanish Civil War.* Berkeley: University of California Press, 1957.

Cleugh, James. *Spain in the Modern World.* London: Eyre & Spottiswoode, 1952.

Colodny, Robert G. *The Struggle for Madrid.* New York: Paine-Whitman, 1958.

Conchon, Georges. *The Measure of Victory.* New York: Orion Press, 1961.

Corwin, Norman. *They Fly Through the Air*. New York: Henry Holt, 1942.

Crossman, Richard, ed. *The God That Failed*. New York: Harper & Bros., 1949.

Deacon, Ruth. *Spain 1937* [n.p., n.d.] Mimeographed copy in the New York Public Library.

Dos Passos, John. *Adventures of a Young Man*. New York: Harcourt, Brace, 1937.

————. *The Great Days*. New York: Sagamore Press, 1958.

————. *Number One*. Boston: Houghton Mifflin Co., 1943.

————. *The Theme Is Freedom*. New York: Dodd, Mead, 1956.

Elliott, Robert C. *The Power of Satire: Magic, Ritual, Art*. Princeton: Princeton University Press, 1960.

Elston, Peter. *Spanish Prisoner*. New York: Carrick & Evans, 1939.

Evenson, Norman. *Camaradas*. New York: Friends of the Abraham Lincoln Brigade [n.d.]

Fox, Ralph. *A Writer in Arms*. New York: International Publishers, 1937.

Ford, Hugh D. *A Poet's War: British Poets and the Spanish Civil War*. Philadelphia: University of Pennsylvania Press, 1965.

Frank, Waldo. *Virgin Spain*. New York: Boni & Liveright, 1942.

Fremantle, Anne. *By Grace of Love*. New York: Macmillan Co., 1957.

Geismar, Maxwell. *Writers in Crisis: The American Novel Between Two Wars*. Boston: Houghton Mifflin Co., 1942.

Gray, James. *On Second Thought*. Minneapolis: University of Minnesota Press, 1946.

Greene, Graham. *The Confidential Agent*. New York: The Viking Press, 1939.

Grieve, Christopher (pseud. Hugh MacDiarmid). *The Battle Continues*. Edinburgh: Castle Wynd Printers, 1957.

Guttmann, Allen. *The Wound in the Heart: America and the Spanish Civil War*. Glencoe, Ill.: The Free Press of Glencoe, 1962.

Hart, Henry, ed. *The Writer in a Changing World*. New York: The Equinox Press, 1937.

Heggen, Thomas. *Mister Roberts*. Boston: Houghton Mifflin Co., 1946.

Hemingway, Ernest. *Death in the Afternoon*. New York: Charles Scribner's Sons, 1932.

————. *A Farewell to Arms*. New York: Charles Scribner's Sons, 1929.

————. *The Fifth Column and the First Forty-Nine Stories*. New York: Charles Scribner's Sons, 1938. Reissued as *The Short Stories of Ernest Hemingway*. New York: The Modern Library [n.d.]

————. *For Whom the Bell Tolls*. New York: Charles Scribner's Sons, 1940.

————. *The Spanish Earth*. Cleveland: J. B. Savage, 1938.

————. *The Spanish War*. London: Fact, 1938.

————. *The Sun Also Rises*. New York: Charles Scribner's Sons, 1926.

————. and others. *Somebody Had to Do Something*. Los Angeles: James Lardner Memorial Fund, 1939.

Hoffman, Frederick J. *The Mortal No: Death and the Modern Imagination*. Princeton: Princeton University Press, 1964.

Hollis, Christopher. *A Study of George Orwell*. London: Hollis & Carter, 1956.

Hopkinson, Tom. *George Orwell*. London: The British Book Council and the National Book League, 1953.

Howe, Irving. *Politics and the Novel*. New York: Meridian Press, 1957.

Hughes, Langston. *I Wonder as I Wander*. New York: Rinehart & Co., 1956.

Jellinek, Frank. *The Civil War in Spain*. London: Victor Gollancz, 1937.

Johnston, Nancy. *Hotel in Spain*. London: Faber & Faber, 1937.

Kaghan, Theodore. *Dear People*. New York: [n.p., n.d.].

————. *Hello Franco*. Typescript in the New York Public Library.

Kazin, Alfred. *On Native Grounds*. Garden City: Doubleday & Co., 1956.

Kempton, Murray. *Part of Our Time: Some Monuments and Ruins of the Thirties*. New York: Simon & Schuster, 1955.

Knoblaugh, H. Edward. *Correspondent in Spain*. New York, London: Sheed & Ward, 1937.

Koestler, Arthur. *Invisible Writing*. London: Collins; Hamish Hamilton, 1954.

————. *The Scum of the Earth*. New York: Macmillan Co., 1941.

————. *Spanish Testament*. London: Victor Gollancz, 1937.

Langdon-Davies, John. *Behind the Spanish Barricades*. London: Secker & Warburg, 1937.

Lawson, John Howard. *Blockade*. Hollywood: United Artists, 1938 (film script).

Lehmann, John. *The Whispering Gallery*. New York: Harcourt, Brace, 1955.

Lewis, Cecil Day. *Collected Poems*. London: Jonathan Cape, 1954.

Lewis, Wyndham. *The Revenge for Love*. Chicago: Henry Regnery, 1952.

Longstreet, Stephen (David Ormsbee). *Chico Goes to the Wars*. New York: E. P. Dutton, 1943.

McCaffery, John K. M., ed. *Ernest Hemingway: The Man and His Work*. Cleveland: World Publishing Co., 1950.

McCullagh, Francis. *In Franco's Spain*. London: Burns Oates, 1937.

MacKee, Seumas. *I Was a Franco Soldier*. London: United Editorial, 1938.

Madariaga, Salvador de. *Spain: A Modern History*. New York: Frederick Praeger, 1958.

Mailer, Norman. *The Naked and the Dead*. New York: Rinehart & Co., 1948.

Malraux, André. *Man's Hope*. New York: Random House, 1938.

Marshall, Bruce. *The Fair Bride*. Boston: Houghton Mifflin, 1953.

Marzani, Carl. *The Survivor*. New York: Cameron Associates, 1958.

Maschler, Tom, ed. *Declaration*. London: MacGibbon & Kee, 1957.

Matthews, Herbert. *Two Wars and More to Come*. New York: Carrick & Evans, 1938.

Muggeridge, Malcolm. *The Sun Never Sets*. New York: Random House, 1940.

Nelson, Steve. *The Volunteers*. New York: International Publishers, 1953.

Norman, James. *The Fell of Dark*. Philadelphia, New York: J. B. Lippincott, 1960.

North, Joseph. *Men in the Tanks*. Foreword by Ernest Hemingway. New York: International Publishers, 1939.

O'Connor, William Van, ed. *Forms of Modern Fiction*. Minneapolis: University of Minnesota Press, 1948.

O'Donnell, Peadar. *Salud! An Irishman in Spain*. London: Methuen, 1937.

Orwell, George. *Homage to Catalonia.* Boston: Beacon Press, 1952 (originally published in London: Secker & Warburg, 1938).

———. *Such, Such Were the Joys.* New York: Harcourt, Brace, 1952.

Osborne, John. *Look Back in Anger.* London: Faber & Faber, 1938.

Paul, Elliott. *The Life and Death of a Spanish Town.* New York: Random House, 1937.

Payne, Robert, ed. *The Civil War in Spain.* New York: G. P. Putnam's Sons, 1962.

———. *The Song of the Peasant.* London: William Heinemann, 1939.

Quintanilla, Luis, Elliott Paul and Jay Allen. Preface by Ernest Hemingway. *All the Brave.* New York: Modern Age, 1939.

Read, Herbert. *Poetry and Anarchism.* London: Faber & Faber, 1938.

Regler, Gustav. *The Great Crusade.* New York: Longmans, Green & Co., 1940.

———. *The Owl of Minerva.* New York: Farrar, Straus & Cudahy, 1959.

Replogle, Justin M. *The Auden Group: The 1930's Poetry of W. H. Auden, C. Day Lewis and Stephen Spender.* Ph.D. dissertation, University of Wisconsin, 1956.

Rideout, Walter B. *The Radical Novel in the United States, 1900–1954.* Cambridge: Harvard University Press, 1956.

Riesenfeld, Janet. *Dancer in Madrid.* New York: Funk & Wagnalls, 1938.

Rolfe, Edwin. *The Lincoln Battalion.* New York: Veterans of the Abraham Lincoln Brigade, 1939.

———. *First Love and Other Poems.* Los Angeles: Larry Edmunds Bookshop, 1951.

Rollins, William, Jr. *The Wall of Men.* New York: Modern Age, 1938.

Romilly, Esmond. *Boadilla.* London: Hamish Hamilton, 1937.

Rukeyser, Muriel. *A Turning Wind.* New York: Covici Friede, 1939.

———. *U.S. 1.* New York: Covici Friede, 1938.

Schochen, Seyril. *I Am Ashamed* [n.p., n.d.]. Typescript in New York Public Library.

Scott-Watson, Keith. *Single to Spain.* London: Arthur Barker, 1937.

Sedwick, Frank. *The Tragedy of Manuel Azana and the Fate of the Spanish Republic.* Columbus: Ohio State University Press, 1963.

Sencourt, Robert. *Spain's Ordeal*. London: Longmans, Green & Co., 1939.

Sender, Ramon. *War in Spain*. London: Faber & Faber, 1937.

Shaw, Irwin. "Main Currents in American Thought," in *Mixed Company*. New York: Random House, 1939.

———. *The Young Lions*. New York: Random House, 1948.

Sheean, Vincent. *Not Peace But A Sword*. London: Arthur Barker; New York: Doubleday & Co., 1939.

Sholley, Hazel. *Night Falls on Spain*. Boston: Bakers Plays, 1939.

Sinclair, Upton. *No Pasarán!* Pasadena: Upton Sinclair, 1937

Slater, Humphrey. *The Heretics*. New York: Harcourt, Brace & Co., 1947.

Solomon, H. Eric. *Studies in 19th Century War Fiction*. Ph.D. dissertation, Harvard, 1957.

Sommerfield, John. *Volunteer in Spain*. New York: Alfred A. Knopf, 1937.

Spender, Stephen. *Collected Poems, 1928–1953*. New York: Random House, 1955.

———. *World Within World*. New York: Harcourt, Brace & Co., 1951.

——— and John Lehmann, eds. *Poems for Spain*. London: Hogarth Press, 1939.

Sprigg, Christopher St. John (Christopher Caudwell). *Illusion and Reality*. New York: International Publishers, 1937.

Stavis, Barrie. *Refuge*. New York: Samuel French, 1939.

Taggard, Genevieve. *Collected Poems, 1918–1938*. New York: Harper & Bros., 1938.

———. *The Long View*. New York: Harper & Bros., 1942.

Taylor, F. Jay. *The United States and the Spanish Civil War*. New York: Bookman Associates, 1956.

Thomas, Hugh. *The Spanish Civil War*. London: Eyre & Spottiswoode, 1961.

Todrin, Boris. *At the Gates*. Prairie City, Illinois: James Decker, 1944.

Toynbee, Philip. *The Barricades*. Garden City: Doubleday, Doran, 1944.

Westerman, Percy F. *Under Fire in Spain*. Glasgow: Blackie & Son, 1937.

Wet, Oloff de. *The Patrol Is Ended*. New York: Doubleday & Co., 1938.

Williams, Oscar, ed. *The War Poets*. New York: John Day, 1945.

Wilson, Edmund. *The American Earthquake*. Garden City: Doubleday Anchor Books, 1958.

———. *Eight Essays*. Garden City: Doubleday Anchor Books, 1954.

———. *The Shores of Light*. New York: Farrar, Straus & Young, 1952.

———. *The Wound and the Bow*. New York: Oxford University Press, 1947.

Writers Take Sides. New York: League of American Writers, 1938.

Yeats, William Butler. *Collected Poems*. New York: Macmillan Co., 1956.

Zglinitzki, Baroness de (Helen Nicholson). *The Painted Bed*. Indianapolis: Bobbs-Merrill, 1938.

PERIODICALS

Backman, Melvin. "The Matador and the Crucified," *Modern Fiction Studies*, I (August, 1955), 31–35.

Barea, Arturo. "Not Spain but Hemingway," *Horizon*, III (May, 1941), 350–61.

Benet, William Rose. "Catalonia," *New Masses*, XXVII (May 31, 1938), 19.

Berryman, John. "Two Poems," *Kenyon Review*, I (Summer, 1939), 257–59.

Cavero de Carondelet, Anna. "Letter to the Editor," *The New York Times Book Review*, LXIII (March 9, 1958), 36.

Cornford, John. "A Letter from Aragon," *Left Review*, II (December, 1936), 771.

Fearing, Kenneth. "The Program," *New Masses*, XXVIII (September 6, 1938), 20.

Graves, Robert. "A Life Bang-Full of Kicks and Shocks," in *The New York Times Book Review*, LXIII (January 5, 1958), 6.

Guttmann, Allen. "Mechanized Doom: Ernest Hemingway and the Spanish Civil War," *The Massachusetts Review*, I (May, 1960), 541–61.

Hellman, Lillian. "A Bleached Lady," *New Masses*, XXIX (October 11, 1938), 20–21.

Hemingway, Ernest. "The Butterfly and the Tank,"*Esquire*, X (December, 1938), 51.

———. "Call for Greatness," *Ken*, I (July 14, 1938), 23.

———. "The Cardinal Picks a Winner," *Ken*, I (May 5, 1938), 38

———. "The Denunciation," *Esquire*, X (November, 1938), 39.

———. "Dying, Well or Badly," *Ken*, I (April 21, 1938), 68.

———. "False News to the President," *Ken*, II (September 8, 1938), 17–18.

———. "Fresh Air on an Inside Story," *Ken*, II (September 22, 1938), 28.

———. "Good Generals Hug the Line," *Ken*, II (August 25, 1938), 28.

———. "H. M.'s Loyal State Department," *Ken*, I (June 16, 1938), 36.

———. "The Next Outbreak of Peace," *Ken*, III (January 12, 1939), 12–13.

———. "The Night Before Battle," *Esquire*, XI (February, 1939), 27–29.

———. "Nobody Ever Dies," *Cosmopolitan*, CVI (March, 1939), 29.

———. "The Old Man at the Bridge," *Ken*, I (May 19, 1938), 36. Printed in *The Short Stories* as "Old Man at the Bridge."

———. "On the American Dead in Spain," *New Masses*, XXX (February 14, 1939), 3.

———. "A Program for U.S. Realism," *Ken*, II (August 11, 1938), 26.

———. "The Time Now, The Place Spain," *Ken*, I (April 7, 1938), 36–37.

———. "Treachery in Aragon," *Ken*, I (June 30, 1938), 26.

———. "United We Fall Upon *Ken*," *Ken*, I (June 2, 1938), 38.

———. "Under the Ridge," *Cosmopolitan*, CVII (October, 1938), 34.

Herbst, Josephine. "The Starched Blue Sky of Spain," *The Noble Savage*, I (March, 1960), 76–117.

Hodgkin, T. L. "Novels and Social Change," *Left Review*, III (December, 1937), 690–92.

Hughes, Langston. "Air Raid: Barcelona," *Esquire*, VIII (October, 1936), 40.

Humphries, Rolfe. "A Gay People," *New Republic*, XCVIII (April 12, 1939), 275.

Kirk, Russell. "The Last of the Scalds," *Sewanee Review*, LXIV (Winter, 1956), 164–70.

Lindsay, Jack. "On Guard for Spain," *Left Review*, III (March, 1937) 81–84.

———. "A Plea for Mass Declamation," *Left Review*, III (October, 1937), 511–17.

Mazer, Milton. "Problem for Today," *The New Yorker*, XX (February 19, 1944), 20–21.

Mellers, William H. "The Ox in Spain," *Scrutiny*, X (June, 1941), 93–99.

Millay, Edna St. Vincent. "Say That We Saw Spain Die," *Harper's*, CLXXVII (October, 1938), 449–52.

Parker, Dorothy. "Soldiers of the Republic," *The New Yorker*, XIII (February 5, 1938), 13–14.

Read, Herbert. "Poetry in My Time," *The Texas Quarterly*, I (February, 1958), 87–100.

Rexroth, Kenneth. "Requiem for the Dead in Spain," *New Republic*, XC (March 24, 1937), 201.

Rukeyser, Muriel. "Mediterranean," *New Masses*, XXIV (September 14, 1937), 18–20.

Sanders, David. "Ernest Hemingway's Spanish Civil War Experiences," *American Quarterly*, XII (Summer, 1960), 133–43.

Spender, Stephen. "New Poetry," *Left Review*, III (July, 1937), 358–61.

Wain, John. "Orwell in Perspective," *New World Writing 12*. New York: New American Library of World Literature, 1957.

Whittridge, Arnold. "English Poetry and the Spanish Civil War," *The Dalhousie Review*, No. 19 (Halifax, N.S., January, 1940), pp. 456–66.

Index

205